W9-DAO-588

DATE DUE

JUN 0 4 1994		

THE EMPRESS CATHERINE

CATHERINE THE GREAT

GERTRUDE ARETZ

THE EMPRESS CATHERINE

LONDON
GODFREY & STEPHENS LTD

PUBLISHED IN 1947 BY GODFREY & STEPHENS LTD.
3/4 CLEMENTS INN, LONDON W.C. 2

COVER DESIGN BY EVADNE ROWAN
TRANSLATION BY HARRY C. SCHNUR

CONTENTS

LIST OF ILLUSTRATIONS

CHAPTER I

Youth

"To TELL THE TRUTH, I never considered myself very beautiful, but I was pleasing, and this was my strong point", wrote Catherine of herself. And pleasing she was—especially to men. Yet all who came near her, with few exceptions, were fascinated by her strong personality and her generous sympathies. The older this extraordinary woman grew, the greater became the number of her friends; her faults, her passions and all her frailties met with universal forgiveness. Vain and coquettish, changing her lovers at a moment's whim, she remained to her contemporaries a genius and a great ruler. Posterity was to become less indulgent; Voltaire's prophecy, that it was not going to quarrel with the Empress, remained unfulfilled. Harsh condemnation has been meted out to her, whilst her character was judged unfairly. Madame de Choiseul, one of the few who already in Catherine's lifetime professed her failure to understand how such a "monster" could cause so much adoration, was told in 1767 by her friend, Voltaire: "There is a woman who has acquired fame. She is the Semiramis of the North, who mobilizes fifty thousand men in order to re-establish tolerance and conscience in Poland . . . I may boast to you that I stand rather in the good graces of the Empress; I am her knight towards and against all. I know well that she is reproached for several small matters concerning her husband. Those are family affairs in which

I do not mix. Besides, it is well if one has a wrong to repair: then one has to make great efforts to win public respect and admiration. Certainly her dreadful husband would not have accomplished one of the great things which my Catherine does every day."

In these wise words the Philosopher of Verney not only cleverly alludes to "his" Catherine's frailties, but also, perhaps unwittingly, lays bare the motive power behind the woman's actions. She wanted to please—and she had to please, for she had much to atone for. Ambition, vanity and sensuality were her strongest passions; charm, gaiety and goodness, her feminine virtues. Even her love affairs were thus distinguished. Never did she arouse repulsion in the men around her, even when she had reached an age when her charms, unlike those of a Ninon de Lenclos or Diane de Poitiers, had ceased to evoke admiration or desire.

Catherine's almost masculine lack of restraint is not entirely due to natural inclination; it must in part have been due to the conditions surrounding her. She might have become a different woman morally, had she begun by finding a great love to fill all her being and to appeal to a nature that was open to every good influence. She was a woman who might have been guided by love truly great, truly pure; but her rashness led her into paths that might have ended in the gutter, had she been living on a different level of society. But she was the Empress, an autocrat with unlimited power over her empire and her court. This may not justify the immorality of her life, but it explains much. A fourteen-year old German princess, a mere child, brought up on the strictest of moral and religious principles and in an atmosphere of almost bourgeois simplicity, is suddenly snatched away and placed amid the semi-asiatic splendour of Empress Elizabeth's court, with its gorgeous, barbarian luxury, debauchery of all kinds, with love affairs carried

on in secret or openly. All this unrolling dazzlingly before
the amazed eyes of an inexperienced child. The Empress
Elizabeth, before whom populace and courtiers would kow-
tow as to a goddess, made no secret of her loose morals, her
undignified love affairs, nor of the almost perpetual state
of drunkenness in which she, and her maids of honour,
were to be seen. And in the midst of this—a little German
girl, the Princess Sophie Auguste Friederike of Anhalt-
Zerbst. To wed a boy, yet a boy corrupt before he had
attained manhood. The first thing he told her were his
amorous adventures; he continued them even after they
were married. Always drunk, both brutal and childish, he
would play with dolls and toy soldiers, or fill the marital
bedchamber with a pack of huge dogs. "There is nothing
worse", Catherine later wrote to Madame Bjelke, "than to
be married to a child. I am one of those who believe that
it is always the husband's fault if his wife fails to love him;
for I would have loved mine most truly, had he been but
good enough to desire me to do so."

Her view may not necessarily be true in all circumstances,
but in her own case it applied. Catherine was left to her
own devices. The court offered little of interest. The women
around her possessed barely an average education, and
even less nobility of soul. The only one to be her mental
equal, the young Princess Dashkov, Catherine was to meet
later. So there remained only the men to appeal to her keen
mind; and though Elizabeth's male courtiers may not have
been much more intelligent than the women, Catherine, in
her conversation with them, felt the added attraction of
sex. "From my fifteenth to my thirty-third year", she
wrote in 1766 to the same Madame Bjelke, "I never really
had the opportunity to converse with women; I had only ladies' maids about me. When I wished to speak with anyone, I
had to go into another room where there were only men.

So it is due partly to habit and partly to my taste that I really understand how to carry on a conversation with men." In the same intensely feminine way she tells us in her Memoirs how first as a Grand Duchess she succumbed to temptation. "I pleased the men, and as the first half of temptation was there, the second followed the first according to human nature; for to tempt and be tempted are very close to each other. And if a strong feeling is added to this, however strongly the principles of morality may be embedded in the mind, one goes farther than one would have wished, and even now"—at the age of fifty!—"I do not know how that is to be prevented. Flight might bring aid, but there are cases, situations, circumstances in life when flight is impossible. How can one in the midst of Court life flee, remove oneself, turn aside? That would at once attract attention and cause talk. Yet if one cannot remove oneself, nothing is harder in my opinion than not to yield to that which allures. All that is said to the contrary is hypocrisy and ignorance of the human heart—the heart, which we do not hold in our hand, to make it obey the dictates of reason."

This is frank enough. Few women have had the courage so openly to search their heart and admit their weakness. And her is another of Catherine's virtues: never does she try to hide her natural inclinations; she is no hypocrite. Coquettish, reckless, abandoned, insatiable in love—but never hypocritical, never content with half measures. In the end it became her habit to satisfy her sensuality; and since the Empress had merely to command, age put no term to her lusts. Soon she became as licentious as any male Don Juan. That such matters should be judged by different moral standards is due, not to some fundamental distinction between both sexes, but to the influence of custom, education, morals and surroundings. Once a woman has burst the barriers and feels no longer bound by the modesty imposed upon her sex, she is likely to act very much as a man would. There have been queens and princesses who indulged in favouritism more openly, more shamelessly and on a larger scale than the most notorious male monarch —and they were not always autocrats who, like Catherine, had no one to fear, not even public opinion. Russia was a country of unlimited possibilities. Catherine was eager not to diminish the glory of her country, but there were no limits to what she could do. The whole of Europe worshipped her and sang her praises, while she sat enthroned in the midst of her people and a brilliant, luxury-loving court, an object of obeisance by millions of her subjects.

Yet there had been a time when that mighty Empress was an insignificant little princess, called to the vast empire of the Czars by a mere chance and raised to the throne by an act of violence which might have miscarried.

Catherine's childhood, like that of all great men and women, is wrapped in the mysterious web of legend. Absurd stories have been told of her descent; there has been mention of a father who would never publicly admit his role— no less a person than Frederick the Great. A genius like Catherine must be sired by a genius. Yet Frederick, still under his father's harsh rod and treated like a truant schoolboy rather than a man, was barely seventeen when Catherine was born! Mention is also made of a young Russian, one Ivan Betzky, a natural son of Prince Trubetskoy, and a favourite of Elizabeth. Catherine's mother met Betsky in Paris; he spent his old age at Catherine's Court, receiving her bounty.

Catherine's mother, the Princess Johanna Elizabeth of Anhalt-Zerbst, may admittedly not have been over strict in matters of marital fidelity. Yet as she had been married for only a year when, at the age of seventeen, she bore

Catherine, we are entitled to dismiss these rumours as mere talk, and to assume that Catherine was indeed the legitimate daughter of Prince Christian August of Anhalt-Zerbst. As confirmed by a letter, written by her father on May 2nd, 1729, she was born on that date, at half-past two in the morning.

The birth of a little princess was no world-shaking event. Her family was neither wealthy nor famed among the princely houses of Germany. The Anhalt-Zerbsts were one of eight branches of the Princes of Anhalt; all of them were to lapse in 1793. At the time of Catherine's birth her father was serving the King of Prussia as Governor of Stettin, and there the little Princess Sophie spent most of her childhood amid the monotony of garrison life. As Empress, she would later jokingly refer to her humble beginnings. When Baron Grimm, her loyal correspondent and adviser, in later years conceived the idea of visiting the place of his beloved Empress's childhood, she wrote to him in jesting mood: "What do you want there? You are not going to find anyone ... But if you insist, know then that I was born in Greiffenheim's house, by St. Mary's church-yard, and that I lived and was brought up in the left wing of the castle; I occupied three vaulted rooms next to the church, and the bell-tower adjoined my bed-chamber. There Mademoiselle Cardel instructed and Herr Wagner examined me. Twice or thrice daily I would from there run to my mother, who dwelt at the other end of the castle. All this is completely devoid of interest, unless you were to have a notion that the locality may have some influence on the production of tolerable empresses. In such case you might advise the King of Prussia to turn it into a kind of boarding school for princesses."

Nothing, then, seemed to prepare little Princess Sophie for a great destiny which neither she nor her parents could

have dreamed of. True, there was some kind of relationship between the modest Princes of Anhalt-Zerbst and the
mighty Russian empire; yet nobody had an inkling that
this relationship would have a decisive influence on the
family's history. Sophie's mother was a Holstein-Gottorp
by birth. A Prince of Holstein-Gottorp had married Anna,
the daughter of Peter the Great and the sister of Empress
Elizabeth, while another Holstein, Karl August, the brother
of Princess Johanna Elizabeth of Anhalt-Zerbst and thus
Sophie's uncle, had been engaged to the then Grand Duchess
Elizabeth of Russia twenty years before. He died, however,
of smallpox shortly before the wedding.

Inscrutable are the ways of destiny. Fike, or Fikchen,
as she was called in the family circle, was destined for
greatness. Yet at first the child did not appear particularly
promising. She learned her lessons well enough, but her
education did not exceed the level considered adequate for
the women of the minor German nobility. Sophie describes
herself as stubborn and lackadaisical and must have caused
many a heartache to her governess, Mademoiselle Cardel. Sophie's mother, young, reckless and emotional, was incapable
of bringing up her daughter, on whom she bestowed more
cuffs than caresses. She was unable to develop her daughter's latent talents and capabilities. Baroness Printzen, later
Sophie's lady-in-waiting, did not hesitate to declare that
she noticed in her just an ordinary character, distinguished
neither by special qualities nor talents; the one thing that
impressed her was "a serious, calculating and cold personality," Catherine later took care of her own education in
Russia, and states, not without some of the pride of the
self-made woman: "I was brought up to become the wife
of some neighbouring princeling, and I was taught just as
much as I needed. I and Mademoiselle Cardel would never
have dreamed of the fate that awaited us."

That fate overtook little Spohie suddenly and unexpectedly, like a bolt from the blue. On December 9, 1741, the news spread through Europe: Grand Duchess Elizabeth of Russia, the daughter of Peter the Great, by one of the sudden coups d'état already traditional in Russia, had put an end to the 'reign' of the infant Czar, Ivan VI, and the regency of his mother, and proclaimed herself Empress. The memory of her deceased betrothed had always caused her to preserve some attachment to the House of Holstein-Gottorp. Yet the world was astonished when, one year after mounting the throne, she called to Russia her fourteen-year old nephew, Prince Karl Peter Ulrich of Holstein-Gottorp, the son of her sister Anna Petrovna, and solemnly designated him heir to the throne. Fike's mother was extremely proud of this distinction conferred on a close relative, the more so as some glory was reflected on her own family. For Frederick the Great in 1749 made Prince Christian August of Anhalt-Zerbst a Field-Marshal—no doubt with the intention of pleasing the Empress Elizabeth.

In 1742 Princess Sophie accompanied her mother to Berlin, where the famous painter, Pesne, painted her portrait. This, too, was done at the instance of Frederick, who wanted the portrait for the Empress of Russia. But a whole year was to pass before Sophie's fate was to be decided. In the meantime the principality of Zerbst had passed to Christian August's brother, Prince Johann Ludwig, and the whole family assembled there for Christmas in 1743. They celebrated their newly-found prosperity. The New Year was hailed with equal gaiety, and began with a good augury for the family.

After matins in the palace chapel the little principality found itself in a flutter of excitement: a courier arrived from Berlin, with a letter from the Grand Duke's Governor, Brümmer, which he handed to Sophie's mother. In this letter, Empress Elizabeth invited mother and daughter to visit the Russian Court. They were to get ready for the journey at once and to travel by the shortest route, first to Petersburg and then to Moscow, where Elizabeth and her Court were then in residence.

Against the expenses of the journey the Empress had opened for them a credit with a Berlin bank to the amount of 10,000 roubles; but this sum was only to cover their costs to the Russian border. In Russia the two ladies and their retinue would be well looked after. They were also requested to reduce their train to the absolute minimum. At Riga, a guard of honour would meet them and escort them to the Imperial residence. Brümmer enjoined the strictest secrecy: Princess Johanna Elizabeth must discuss the journey with no one—not even her own husband. Only in Frederick the Great was she allowed to confide. He was 'in the know', for only a few hours later a letter arrived from him, mentioning a possible marriage between young Sophie and Grand Duke Peter. Frederick subsequently claimed most of the credit for the whole plan; but then he much preferred to see Sophie on the throne of Russia rather than Princess Marianne of Saxony, a daughter of August III, King of Poland. Frederick might have given his own sister in marriage to the Grand Duke, Elizabeth not being averse to this union; but the idea seemed so absurd to the King of Prussia that he remarked: "Nothing would be more unnatural than to sacrifice the Princess for interest and ambition". His beloved sister was too good for barbarian Russia. Let some insignificant little princess be found to take her place, one who would be overjoyed at such a brilliant match—and one who was not likely to become a political danger. The Great Catherine thus owes her destiny, however indirectly, to the greatest genius and rival among her contemporaries.

There was no time to be lost. The powerful Empress's wish was a command. Letters upon letters came from Berlin, from Frederick and from Brümmer, urging immediate departure. Fike's luxury-loving mother wished for wings to fly as fast as possible to the brilliant court of Russia. In anticipation she savoured the dazzling galas, the splendour and wealth that awaited her at Elizabeth's court. However, some preparation was required for the journey, even if there was no time left to equip Sophie adequately for Petersburg and Moscow. Three dresses, a dozen chemises and as many stockings and handkerchiefs were all the young Princess had to pack. The Empress had promised to take care of everything, once they had set foot on Russian soil, so no one worried—least of all Sophie's mother. She thought only of herself and of the success she was going to be at court; she also envisaged some political activity by which she might show her gratitude to Frederick.

Sophie was told no more concerning the journey than that it was a routine invitation from relatives. Yet among the nobility such journeys always have their special reasons, and Sophie may have guessed the truth.

When she left Zerbst on January 12, 1744, everything indicated a prolonged absence. Her uncle, the reigning Prince, bade her an emotional farewell, presenting her with a beautiful piece of silver cloth for a court dress; while her father, a strict Protestant, had tears in his eyes as he pressed upon her a weighty tome, written by the learned Heineccius. It was a treatise on the Greek Church which, her father whispered with an air of mystery, she might require one day. This book, Christian August thought, would protect her against insidious influences. As Frederick wrote in a subsequent letter: "My good Prince of Zerbst was very restive on this point; I had a great deal of trouble in overcoming his religious scruples. He responded to all my representations with: '*Meine Tochter soll nicht Griech-isch werden*' (my daughter shall not turn Greek). But a clergyman whom I managed to persuade was complaisant enough to convince him that the Greek and Lutheran chur-ches had very much in common, and now he repeated: '*Lutherisch-Griechisch, Lutherisch-Griechisch, das gehet an*' (Lutheran-Greek, very well)." Christian August's daugh-ter, brought up on strict Lutheran principles, not only be-came an apparently ardent convert to the Russian Church, but at the same time one of the most advanced atheists ever to wear a crown.

Sophie's father also felt it necessary to furnish her with good advice and admonitions for the journey, especially as he had little confidence in his wife who had no such qualms of conscience, basking only in the bliss of being honoured by the Empress. The Prince therefore had penned a long document, entitled 'Pro Memoria'. The young Princess was to read it when the time came. In these instructions he exhorted her to show the greatest deference and obedience to those who were going to make her fortune. The happi-ness of her Lord was to be her supreme purpose; she was not to become familiar with anyone in her entourage; to take charge of her own pocket money, so as not to become dependent upon some servant; and not to meddle in public affairs. The Prince expressed himself in a curiously stilted mixture of German and French, advising her "not to enter into *familiarité* or badinage, but always to conserve some *égards*; not to enter into affairs of government, so as not to exacerbate the Senate". We shall soon see how the young Princess reacted to these paternal admonitions; they form an amusing contrast to her subsequent activities in politics —and elsewhere.

Yet Sophie was only setting out on her road to fortune. Her route led to Berlin, where she met the King for the

last time, and then, viâ Stargard, Memel and Mitau, to
Riga. It was a long and arduous journey in mid-winter. The
ladies travelled under an assumed name, as the Countesses
Reinbeck. Fikchen's mother found the fatigues of the journey hard to bear, whilst the girl, young and vigorous, hardly felt the strain: there were so many new things to see.
At long last they reached Riga, where a splendid reception
rewarded them for the rigour of the journey. From now on
they made a veritable royal progress. In her letters to her
husband, Johanna Elizabeth hardly finds words adequate
to describe the luxury, the splendour, the respectful homage
shown to them. Immense wealth, a foretaste of the brilliance of the Imperial Court, dazzled and intoxicated them.
Richly furnished apartments, footmen at every door, couriers and lackeys thronging the stairs; in brightly lit and
ornate salons the cream of Russian and Baltic nobility. All
the paraphernalia of a brilliant court, colourful uniforms
magnificent gowns, women, beautiful, amiable, decked in
diamonds—and courtly gentlemen bowing deep to Johanna
and Sophie, close relatives of the Empress, and paying them
knightly attention—the Princess felt in a dream when she
wrote to Christian August: "It seems as if I were in the
suite of Her Imperial Majesty or of some great monarch.
It does not seem real that all this should happen to poor
me, for whom hardly a drum was ever stirred anywhere.
Here everything is so magnificent that it seems to me as if
it all were only a dream."

In Mitau Elizabeth had already provided an escort for
the two Princesses. She sent them two comfortable sledges,
each drawn by six horses. Across the snowy plains of
Russia, they flew like the wind to Petersburg. Here they
tarried for three days only, barely time enough to provide
Fikchen with some court dresses. She had to look decent
before Elizabeth, who was known to own 15,000 silk dresses

and 5,000 pairs of shoes. Those three days in Petersburg
were a dazzling chain of galas, glamour and amusement.
Johanna Elizabeth was bedazzled by it all. But young Sophie
seemed less impressed by all this lavish splendour. At the
age of fifteen she already displayed signs of that clear
vision that was later to distinguish the great Empress.
"Fikchen", her mother writes to her father, "sustains the
fatigue better than I. The greatness that surrounds us
seems to support her fortitude."

CHAPTER II

Betrothal in Moscow

SOPHIE AND HER MOTHER travelled from Petersburg to Moscow in tearing haste, resting neither day nor night, for the Empress wished the young Princess to be present at Court on February 21, the Grand Duke's birthday. Sixteen horses were now drawing the Princesses' sledge; it flew like an arrow across the steppe, past villages and hamlets. Furious speed spared neither men nor horses, and the ladies managed to arrive in time at the Galavinsky Dvaretz, the log palace where Elizabeth resided. The Empress was very eager to see the Princess intended for her nephew. From far away, behind a crowd of courtiers, she scrutinised her guests without being noticed by them. The Grand Duke, on the other hand, youthfully eager and curious, forgot all etiquette and dashed into the Princesses' apartments the moment they arrived.

This was not Fikchen's first meeting with her cousin. They had met in 1739, when he was eleven, and she was ten. It was at Eutin, in the house of his guardian, the Archbishop of Lübeck. Peter Ulrich was educated there after the death of his father, Duke Karl Friedrich of Holstein-Gottorp. Even then ten-year old Sophie disliked the pale, skinny, sickly boy to whom his attendants, as she writes in her memoirs, "wished to give the appearance of a man." The boy had a sorry childhood. He received next to no education, and threats and punishment had made him timid and sullen. Many beatings had given him a tendency towards headaches and bouts of vomiting. He had the greatest hatred for his Swedish governor, the later Grand Master of his Court, Brümmer. Some wit said of that pedagogue that he was a good trainer of horses, not of princes. The young Duke was undernourished, too; he had to miss many a meal because people neglected him. Much too early, on the other hand, did his tutor force him to take part in social gatherings, and to dance at every Court ball. Little Sophie heard family gossip, alleging that the boy of eleven was addicted to drink, that he was both obstinate and tempestuous. At Eutin, Peter made a very bad impression on her—so much so that she refused to speak to him. When she met him for the second time in Moscow things were not much better, but she made an effort to overcome her aversion from the sickly-looking young man. She was kind and pleasant to him. Even as a little girl she knew how to make friends and become popular, and now, in Moscow, she understood that an Imperial crown was no mean prospect. Despite her innate modesty she played her part as favourite and future queen as if she had spent her whole youth at a court as brilliant as that of Russia. Despite her tender years she mastered difficult situations arising from her position with complete assurance. *"Elle se plaît aux grandeurs qui l'environnent"* (she delights in the grandeur of her surroundings), her mother wrote to Frederick, while Catherine later says in her memoirs: "As to the Grand Duke, I neither liked him nor disliked him, but the Russian crown meant more to me than he."

Her behaviour at that time gave proof of cool calculation, calm deliberation and a sure touch. From the outset she was mistress of the situation. She was resolved to overcome all difficulties, to make any sacrifice in order not to lose the crown of Russia. There were intrigues and conflicts—

sometimes with her own mother who, still young and vain, treated her in an inconsiderate and imperious manner. From the outset, too, she was swept into the whirl of court intrigue. Chancellor Bestushev, who had favoured an alliance with the Princess of Saxony, was incensed by her arrival and became her enemy. Yet with her own inimitable tact the young Princess knew how to make her way, and even how to turn enemies into friends.

Empress Elizabeth seemed greatly pleased with her choice of a bride for her nephew and heir. She liked Princess Sophie, found her charming and overwhelmed her with proofs of her affection. Soon the whole Court was enchanted by the unspoiled young Princess. Her mother was less popular, as she had immediately entangled herself in imprudent and unskilful political intrigue. Still, Johanna Elizabeth wrote to her husband in Zerbst: "We live here like queens." She did not bother about Sophie's marriage, taking it for granted, although the Empress had as yet failed to mention it openly. "The matter is settled", she wrote some days later. "The Empress spoils, the Grand Duke loves her." She, too, was bedazzled by the crown of Russia, for which she would willingly have sacrificed her daughter's happiness. This mother did not ask what her daughter's feelings for the Grand Duke were: the heart of a princess is mute. Peter was a Grand Duke and was to become an Emperor: greater happiness than this was not looked for.

Despite her youth, Sophie soon realised that this youngster, sickly and already corrupted by the wrong teaching, was not the man to make her happy. He was in utter and miserable contrast to her character and common sense. Peter was impetuous and brutal, but at the same time timid and cowardly; he was boastful, a liar and completely childish. The intelligent girl was more than once amazed at his limitless ignorance and the impudence with which he would boast of martial feats he had never done, and of his numerous love affairs. At sixteen, he claimed to have had many, and had no hesitation in telling her all about them. He said that what pleased him was that Sophie was his cousin: thus he could open his heart to her with entire confidence. The first confession he made to her was that he was in love with one of the Empress's maids-of-honour, a Demoiselle Labukhin. He wanted to marry her, but since his aunt wished him to marry the Princess of Zerbst he had given her up. With these and other stories Peter regaled his bride-to-be, in whom he saw no more than a relative. Yet Sophie had much to make her appear attractive and desirable in the eyes of a young man. Well developed for her age, she was tall and well formed. Soft dark locks, charmingly arranged, surrounded a fresh, pleasant face, with the merry mouth of a child and large, expressive grey eyes. This young girl early developed signs of future attractiveness; but Peter had no eyes for her. His mind was filled with childish games and pastimes, later to be joined by the vice of drink. Sophie would bear his ineptness with good grace, listen to his confidences and sometimes laugh over his imbecilities, for she, too, was still a child, full of high spirits and vivacity. But on the whole she held aloof from Peter. It is surprising how well she was able even then to judge people. She realised at once that she must first of all secure Elizabeth's affection, and there was no better way of doing so than by falling in with all her wishes. She was astounded at Peter's lack of caution and judgment, but profited from it in order to form her own decisions.

In order to establish herself in Russia and play a prominent part in public life, Sophie must first of all become a Russian. This she realized. Peter, on the other hand, disliked the Russian language, the customs of the country and even the Greek Church. No wonder that the Russians did not love him and always considered him a foreigner. "I saw and understood", says Catherine in her memoirs, "that he did not care much for the people he was one day to rule. He retained his Lutheran faith, disliked his surroundings and was a big child." All the greater were her efforts to become popular, and to establish lasting ties with her new country. After one week in Moscow she already had three masters: Simeon Todorsky taught her the Orthodox creed, Vassili Adadurov instructed her in the Russian language, and Monsieur Laudé gave her dancing lessons. The Grand Duke, too, had his instructors; Stählin, his tutor, took special pains with him. He sought to instruct him by way of play, and to teach him the rudiments of history, political economy, mathematics and fortification in an entertaining manner. But Peter was averse to learning; Russian, which he considered too difficult, he did not take up at all.

Young Sophie, on the other hand, was particularly interested in that language. While her future husband wasted his time in childish play with servants, the ambitious little Princess proved greedy for knowledge. In order to make speedier progress she would even get up at night, when everybody else was asleep, dressed only in her night-shift and with bare feet, and read in her Russian grammar. This was in mid-winter and caused her to be seized with a dangerous attack of pleurisy. For a month she hovered between life and death. News of her illness soon spread, not only at the Court but throughout the country and increased the sympathy felt for her. People were touched to hear of this young girl getting up on a wintry night in order to learn the tongue of the people over whom she was one day to reign at her husband's side. The Empress, deeply worried, rushed to her bedside as soon as the news reached her at Troitza Convent, where she was staying with her retinue.

The Court Physician was sent for to treat Sophie: he bled her no fewer than sixteen times within twenty-seven days, in accordance with medical practice in those days. But the fever and pain persisted, and grave concern was felt. Even the Grand Duke was affected and showed his attachment by presenting her with a magnificent watch, studded with diamonds and rubies. Finally her life was despaired of; a priest was about to be summoned. Her mother, thinking her insufficiently initiated into the Greek Church, suggested a Lutheran clergyman; but the sick girl said: "Why? Call Simeon Todorsky rather."

The most calculating, the most expert of actresses could not have produced a better effect than did this sick young girl who followed her natural instinct; this girl who was later to become the fervent admirer, friend and pupil as well as the public partisan of the notorious atheist, Voltaire. This little incident proved very effective: it could not fail to become public property and served to kindle a halo around the shrewd little head of the Grand-Duchess-to-be. The Petersburg press reported that Princess Sophie was devoting several hours each day to her Russian studies, while the daily bulletins on her health stressed the patience and meekness displayed by the sufferer. Sophie's position in Russia was now assured; from now on she could count on the grateful affections of a simple, deeply religious people.

But Todorsky did not have to give her the extreme unction; Sophie's sound, youthful constitution triumphed over the illness. On her fifteenth birthday she was able to get up again for the first time. When she appeared at Court a few days later, she was so deadly pale—"*d'une pâleur mortelle*"—that the Empress sent her a pot of rouge; yet the young Princess would not paint her face—yet. In later years she was to do so to excess, sometimes arousing mocking comment. But despite her pallor, the slim young Princess pleased and became a universal favourite. Her gaiety and charm, her youth and friendliness warmed the frigid air of the court and won everybody's heart. She was pleasant and attractive, not only because of her personal qualities but also by reason of her keen intelligence. The easy grace with which she moved in her new, unwontedly splendid surroundings; the speed with which she mastered the Russian language; the cheerful graciousness of all her sayings and doings, and the kindness and consideration she showed towards everybody, including servants—all this made her many devoted friends. People felt sorry for her in having to marry such a clod—a fact which did not prevent official circles from pretending that here was a case of spontaneous attraction of two loving hearts.

Yet Sophie's destiny very nearly took a different turn, and the crown of Russia might have adorned some other head. Had this happened, it would have been her mother's fault. There occurred stormy incidents between Empress Elizabeth and Princess Johanna who had been unwise enough to intrigue against Elizabeth's Minister and favourite. She was greatly compromised through a correspondence with the French Ambassador, Chétardie, and the foolish woman might have paid dearly for her lapse, had not her daughter enjoyed the Empress's entire confidence. Elizabeth was content to punish the Princess with her contempt; as soon as the wedding was over, she sent her away from Court, and back to Germany. During one such stormy scene, with Johanna in tears and on her knees before the furious Empress, the Grand Duke and Princess Sophie happened to be in a nearby room. Like real children they were laughing and playing on the window-seat when Count Lestocq, the Empress's favourite, suddenly came into the room and rudely told them that their merriment was soon going to stop. Let the Princess pack up; she would return home directly. Describing this scene forty years afterwards, Catherine writes: "I saw that the Grand Duke would have given me up without regret; as for myself, his loss was a matter of indifference to me, but that of the Russian crown was not . . . My heart was full of dread, and only my ambition sustained me."

Ambition, energy and vanity were already fully developed in her. With unequalled application she would devote herself to her Russian studies; with equal eagerness the girl, hitherto a confirmed Lutheran, embraced the Greek faith. "The change of religion", wrote the Prussian Minister, Mardefeld, to his King, "gives the Princess infinite pain, and her tears flow abundantly when she is alone with persons of whom she is not suspicious. Nevertheless ambition is finally gaining the upper hand." Already by June, 1744, however, Sophie had overcome her scruples sufficiently to recite the creed unhesitatingly, in Russian, in the Imperial Chapel of the Moscow Palace. She had learned it so well and recited it with so much devotion and fervour that the Archbishop of Novgorod was in tears when he found such an ardent *blagovyernaya* (orthodox believer) in the Grand Duchess-to-be. All those present shed tears—as they had done at the Grand Duke's conversion, though he had amused himself during the ceremony by making faces and putting out his tongue. No longer was the Princess now the little Sophie, who had demurely crossed the threshold of the Sanctuary with its glittering golden ikons; she left the church as the Grand Duchess Catherine Alexeievna.

Catherine, kneeling devoutly in the chapel and shyly reciting the words: "I believe and confess that faith alone is not sufficient for our justification . . .", was later, as Voltaire's disciple, to scoff at all conversions. When she was expecting her future daughter-in-law, she said: "As soon as we have her here we shall go about her conversion. In order to convince her we shall need about a fortnight. How much time will be needed to teach her to read the Confession of Faith correctly and distinctly in Russian, I do not know." At fifteen, at any rate, Catherine did not make as light of the business as she did at fifty. But then, the Empress rewarded her with a diamond necklace and clasp whose value her businesslike mother put at 100,000 roubles.

The next day, on June 29, the betrothal was celebrated in the Uspiensky Sobor. Catherine was a charming bride who conquered all hearts. She was considered a high-spirited girl, and not without wit. She proved extremely shrewd in making her way. "I showed no marked preference for anybody, did not meddle in affairs, was always gay, complaisant and courteous; and since I was cheerful by nature it gave me great pleasure to notice how I was daily winning the public's esteem ... To my mother I showed great respect, towards the Empress, limitless obedience, towards the Grand Duke, devotion—at least outwardly—and I took the greatest pains to become popular." She acted with the greatest circumspection, doing nothing without previous consideration, while the Grand Duke was "as discreet as a gun shot." One day he informed his bride that his valet had advised him to treat his future wife very strictly. He must never allow her to meddle in his affairs: the man who let his wife dominate him was a poltroon. Another time he sent a lackey to tell her that he was unable to visit her so frequently, as his rooms were too far aways from hers.

Young Catherine had thus ample reason not to expect a happy future with such a boor. Yet although her pride suffered, she complained to no one. Her ambition always gained the upper hand. She would weep bitterly in her room, but if one of her maids surprised her she would not tell the real reason. Even at that time the thought of arousing pity in others was abhorrent to her. Yet the young bride at that period did not lack sorrows and annoyance from other sources. Her mother was unkind and inconsiderate to her and, at the same time, envious and prone to intrigue. One day she went so far as to accuse her own daughter before the Empress of having received the Grand Duke in her room at night. In time, there also came friction with the Empress, who was not always pleased with Catherine. She accused her of extravagant spending and love of finery. On one occasion, when all were in the theatre, the Grand Duchess, her mother and the Grand Duke sharing Peter's box, Catherine noticed the Empress, in her box opposite, haranguing Lestocq and throwing angry looks at her. A few moments later the Empress's favourite entered the Grand Duke's box and, addressing Catherine in an offensive and almost brutal tone, said: "Do you know that the Empress is very angry with you? You are heavily in debt."—There was nothing Catherine could say in reply. True, she had run up debts to the tune of 17,000 roubles in a few months; so she could only cry. Inwardly, however, she felt that the Empress was being unfair to her. Elizabeth was a spendthrift herself, changing her dresses five or six times a day, one more costly than the other; while Catherine, who had come to her lavish court with hardly any clothes at all, had had to buy everything for herself. She had also discovered that in Russia, more than in any other country, people like presents. Even the Grand Duke cost her a lot of money in that respect, for he was very eager for presents. Moreover, the young Grand Duchess elect had been given as principal lady of what was now her own Court the Countess Rumiantzov, who was the greatest spendthrift at court. Surrounded by a swarm of modistes, milliners and tradesmen, she encouraged her equally extravagant mistress to ever greater expenditure.

Catherine's betrothal was no bed of roses. While the Grand Duke neglected his bride, wasting his time in childish amusements, Catherine, on Count Gyllenborg's recommendation, sent for the works of Plutarch, Cicero and Montesquieu. At fifteen, she was as industrious as any mature person, and would often converse with Gyllenborg, a wise and serious-minded man. One day he remarked that he was afraid she did not know herself as yet and might be wrecked on the many rocks surrounding her. Catherine retorted that she knew herself very well indeed and was going to draft a portrait of her mind and character for him. Thereupon she wrote a dissertation entitled: "Attempt at a portrayal of the character of a fifteen-year-old philosopher." She says in her memoirs: "I found the composition again in 1758, and was amazed to see how well I knew already at the age of fifteen the most secret corners of my soul. Count Gyllenborg gave the paper back to me a few days later, accompanied by a dozen pages of remarks and observations by which he endeavoured to strengthen my character and will-power as much as the other qualities of the mind and the heart. I read carefully what he had written, absorbed it and earnestly resolved to follow his advice. I gave that promise to myself, and as far as I recollect I have kept every promise I made to myself. I then gave him back his letter, as he had requested, and I confess that it has served greatly to form and strengthen my mind and my soul." It really seems that Gyllenborg's guidance had a strong influence on Catherine's subsequent development.

Her sojourn in Moscow was coming to an end. Preparations were taken in hand for the nuptials, to be celebrated in Petersburg. The young couple set out for the capital in December, 1744; but Peter had to stop in the village of Chotilovo, being stricken with the smallpox. Full of apprehension, Elizabeth removed the girl and Catherine and her mother continued their journey, while the Empress herself would not budge from the Grand Duke's bed of sickness. Now Catherine had her first opportunity of writing letters to her future husband. They were in Russian, real love letters with all those tender endearments in which the Slav tongues abound. Yet it was not Catherine who composed those tender missives, but her teacher Adadurov. She only copied them. Very likely she did not, at that time, understand half of what she was writing. But the Empress was highly gratified and deeply touched by "the tender attachment between the two children."

It was only in January, 1745, that Peter was able to follow his betrothed to Petersburg. If he had been no beauty before, the smallpox had now marked him so badly that he was quite unrecognisable. His feeble frame had grown even longer and thinner, his face was swollen, inflamed and covered with deep fresh scars. In addition, he was wearing a monstrous wig, having had all his hair cut off during his illness. The poor boy was indeed not likely to make a favourable impression on his bride. Catherine was deeply shocked when she saw him; it took all her courage to embrace and kiss him. But she did.

Ever since her own illness she had blossomed into a charming maiden. The Empress was enchanted with her beauty and charm and told her so when she dined with her alone on the occasion of Peter's birthday, the Grand Duke still being unable to make public appearances. Elizabeth stressed the good taste shown by Catherine in her clothes. She would dress simply, but in exquisite taste. Catherine knew already how to present at best advantage, not only her intellectual capacities but also her appearance. Among the many beautiful women at Court the little German princess had become the object of universal interest on account of her charm and beauty. Peter alone did not care for his bride's loveliness. His aunt wished him to marry this princess, and there was no gainsaying her. Such things as love and affection were not involved. The wedding took place on August 25, 1745, when Catherine was sixteen and Peter just seventeen years old.

CHAPTER III

A Royal Marriage

NEVER HAD PETERSBURG SEEN a wedding as brilliant as that given by Empress Elizabeth for her nephew and his bride. She took as her model similar celebrations in Versailles and Dresden, having sent for detailed descriptions from both these towns. Everybody agreed that they had never seen as splendid a wedding procession as that of Peter and Catherine in Kazan Cathedral. The religious celebration alone took six hours, and for ten days there were fêtes, dances, masked balls, gala dinners, shows, illuminations, fireworks and all sorts of popular entertainments.

When the ten days were over—Catherine and Peter had hardly had a moment together—they took up residence at the Summer Palace with the Empress. Here, Peter barely took notice of his young wife, preferring the company of his valets and lackeys with whom he could smoke and drink. Twenty times a day he would change his uniform to perform puerile military drill with his menials, issuing commands that were both unnecessary and ridiculous. Meanwhile Catherine, utterly bored, sat yawning in her apartments, where she had no one to talk to. All the people she liked had been sent away from her, one by one, for Elizabeth was becoming suspicious. A short time after the wedding Catherine's mother, too, had to go. True, Johanna Elizabeth had not been an ideal mother, but after all she was her mother. Much as Catherine had suffered from her moods and her bent for intrigue, she keenly felt the separation now. A stranger, she was now alone at that great Court. The young Grand Duchess cried, feeling an immense emptiness, a terrible loneliness. Her husband was unable to fill even the small void in her heart left by her mother. He felt not the slightest affection for his wife. A fortnight after the wedding he once again confided his love affairs to her. Now he was honouring another of the Empress's ladies-in-waiting with his attentions—Demoiselle Carr, later the Princess Galitzin. In his wife's presence he would argue with Count Devierre about Demoiselle Carr's charms, putting them a thousandfold above Catherine's. Catherine was again obliged to tell herself that she could expect no happiness from such a man, who did not love her but merely tolerated the woman he had been forced to marry. Yet there was still a sense of duty in the young Grand Duchess, and that feeling might have induced her to be his loyal consort for a number of years. She frequently speaks with bitterness when mentioning that period. "I should have been the most unhappy creature in the world if I had allowed myself to be carried away by feelings of tenderness for him. He would have ill repaid me, and I should have died of jealousy which would have done nobody any good. So I tried to control myself in order not to be jealous of a man who did not love me. But in order not to be jealous there was only one means: not to love him." She adds, a little sarcastically: "If he had wished to be loved, nothing would have been easier for me, for my nature had accustomed me to fulfil my duties. But for this I would have needed a reasonable husband; and Peter was not."

Catherine was, in fact, still a child herself, in need of guidance and care. But her husband, who should have given that guidance, was an even greater child, and moreover morally unsuited to be her support. Even the Empress had to realize that. No paragon herself in any respect, she still had sufficient common sense to judge matters correctly. Nine months after Catherine's and Peter's wedding she gave the young couple two governors—in the strictest meaning of the term. They were to educate the newly-weds, much in whose married life displeased the Empress. Her choice fell on Monsieur and Madame Choglokov, whose marriage was considered exemplary, for Madame Choglokov was faithful to her husband and presented him with offspring at the shortest possible intervals. Yet Elizabeth seems to have overlooked the maturity and independence which Catherine, despite her youth, already possessed. The new guardianship soon degenerated into a pettifogging tutelage over everything the young couple did, completely missing its purpose. Chancellor Bestushev drew up a special document, a kind of memorandum in which he enumerated all the faults of Peter and Catherine that were to be most strictly corrected by the Choglokovs. Peter's list of sins referred mostly to his bad manners, both in church and at Court, and his complete lack of interest in serious pursuits. "The person selected to keep the Grand Duke company", says this curious document on how to bring up Russian Grand Dukes, "will endeavour to reprimand certain unseemly habits of his Imperial Highness. He must not, for instance, when at table pour the contents of his glass over the servants' heads, nor must he address coarse expressions or improper jokes to those who have the honour to come near him, including foreigners of distinction who are received at Court; or publicly make grimaces and continually jerk his limbs." The document further forbids the Grand Duke to be familiar with servants, and finally it says that the Empress finds it hardly credible that he should be playing with toy soldiers and dolls in the Grand Duchess's apartments.

The young Grand Duchess was accused of different faults. She did not go to church often enough, and meddled with affairs of state, both Russian and Holstein. Her greatest fault was, however, her excessive familiarity with young courtiers in her entourage, with the gentlemen-of-the-bed-chamber, the young gentlemen-ushers, the pages, and even the footmen.

In this respect Bestushev was not wrong. Peter was surrounded by numbers of good-looking and gay young officers. Not all of them had a mind for their master's puerilities, his childish playing at soldiers, and his debauches. Some of them even had intelligence, wit and a bent for poetry, and were not averse to a flirtation with the lovely Grand Duchess. Even before Catherine's marriage, an intimate friendship had sprung up between her, the two Chernichev brothers and one of their cousins. They were all "tall and well-built", especially the eldest among them, their cousin Andrei. He was the most accomplished and handsome of the gentlemen around Catherine. Greatly liked by the Grand Duke, he soon became more than a friend to the Grand Duchess. Peter's indifference or obtuseness was such that he failed to notice his bride's familiarity with his young officers. He regarded it all as harmless badinage and even encouraged Chernichev to employ certain tender pet names for the Princess. Peter sometimes overstepped the borders of what was permissible, for he completely lacked the sense to distinguish the seemly from the unseemly. In the end it was Chernichev who had to remind the princely fiancé that the Princess of Anhalt-Zerbst was one day to be Grand Duchess of Russia, and not Madame Chernichev. This observation amused Peter enormously: he roared with laughter and from that day on called the young officer Catherine's betrothed. When discussing the Princess with him he would call her "your intended".

When Catherine was married the flirtation went on. They gave each other pet names, *matushka* (mummy) and *synók* (sonny) so as to make the whole thing appear harmless. Yet Catherine's feelings were not maternal, nor were those of Andrei Chernichev filial. Both of them, being young, were incapable of hiding their mutual attraction. The Grand Duchess's entourage and retinue were quick to guess her secret. Timofei Yefreimov, her valet, one day permitted himself to observe that she was compromising herself with Chernichev. The matter already seemed to have created so much talk that Timofei advised the rash young man to feign illness and keep to his bed for some time. Andrei followed this advice and Catherine was greatly amused to notice the simplicity with which her husband believed in this "*malade malgré lui,*" and how easy it was to deceive the Empress. But Chernichev soon tired of his self-imposed banishment; he thought his illness had lasted long enough, and resumed his former relations with the Grand Duchess. The Duke even aided them unwittingly. He would send Chernichev with messages to his wife, and Andrei, who liked nothing better, increased the number of these pleasant errands by suggesting messages to the Grand Duke several times a day. As Peter was by nature lazy and indolent and disliked leaving his own apartments and pastimes, he welcomed Chernichev's obligingness.

The Duchess was not always surrounded by her ladies when Andrei entered her room. There must have been moments when looks were more eloquent than words. It may be that on that evening when the Chamberlain, Count Devierre, surprised them she had promised him a more private tête-à-tête. Catherine tells the story in a very harmless manner, though there are grounds for doubt. It happened at one of the concerts beloved by the Grand Duke which Catherine, at the Grand Duke's request, was obliged to attend. She was bored to death, not because of the inferior quality of the music but because, being tone deaf, she lacked all appreciation of it. That night she slipped out unobserved and retired to her chamber. All her ladies were at the concert. Her first lady, Madame Kruse, was away visiting her daughter, and the Empress who would at unexpected times send for Catherine in order to have her movements watched, was absent that night. Catherine's room adjoined a large salon. "By the merest chance", she says, "I happened to open my door, and saw at the other end of the hall Andrei Chernichev". But how did he, supposed to be at the Grand Duke's concert, happen to be in the large hall adjoining Catherine's room? What was he doing there? Certainly a peculiar coincidence. Moreover, instead of closing her door she beckoned to Chernichev in order to ask him, as she says, whether the Empress had come back. Chernichev used the subterfuge of telling her that he could not talk with her here: somebody might come at any moment and see them. Would she let him into her room? Catherine, young and venturesome, may have wished for nothing better, but at that moment the other door of the salon opened, and Count Devierre, the Empress's Chamberlain and spy, came in with the message that the Grand Duke wished to see his wife. This time the tryst was foiled.

The following day strait-laced Madame Choglokov began her service with Catherine. From her the Duke and Duchess learned that the three Chernichevs had been removed from Court and sent to join their regiments at Orenburg, in Siberia. This amounted to banishment. Andrei's flirtation was to cost them dear: Andrei even had to spend some time in prison.

Catherine was not a sentimental woman. She knew that she would find another Chernichev whenever she wished. However, she found ways of eluding the Empress's watchers and entering into correspondence with Andrei. This was a boon to her in the terrible boredom reigning at Oranienbaum, where the Court went soon afterwards.

Bestushev's memorandum, however, had other aims than education alone. A royal couple's first duty is to ensure the continuance of the dynasty; yet Catherine showed to signs of being about to produce an heir. It was therefore felt that the two "children's" attention should be drawn to this. The governess was urged "to exhort the Grand Duchess to fall in with her husband's wishes more obediently than hitherto, to show herself complaisant, agreeable, amorous and, if need be, passionate, *in fine,* by all means to strive for her husband's tenderness, and to fulfil her wifely duties."

The fact that the first few years of Catherine's marriage remained childless has given rise to many conjectures. Some modern writers think that Peter must have suffered from physical incapacity. It is, however, an established fact that he had many mistresses, and that his relations with them were far from platonic. The only correct explanation for Catherine's barrenness during the first few years of her married life would appear to be that the two of them, being utterly indifferent to each other, failed to establish marital relations. Catherine herself in her memoirs hints that Paul was not Peter's son. For the time being, at any rate, Catherine gave no thought to motherhood—a sentiment that failed to rouse her even when she later had children by her lovers. She was preoccupied with sensual gratification.

In the monotony of life at Oranienbaum, Catherine found a fresh delight in reading. It is amazing how the young woman managed to preserve her private life with its intellectual and literary bent whilst surrounded by a Court that combined the greatest luxury with coarse manners and licentious behaviour. Neither her husband nor the Empress set her a good example. Elizabeth had no education; she touched no book apart from the Bible and sought no knowledge. Her one talent was a sure hand in selecting her ministers. Lazy and indolent by nature, she loved the pleasures of the table, and especially drink. She would sit drinking deep into the night in the company of her Guards officers or under-officers. She was vain, fond of finery, and shallow, and withal extremely bigoted. She did not lack kindness, but was irascible and moody. The Chevalier d'Eon relates: "When she ascended the throne she swore upon the sacred image of St. Nikolai that no one was going to suffer execution during her reign. And she kept her word— according to the letter. No head fell, but two thousand tongues and two thousand ears were cut off."

The Empress Elizabeth was amorous as well, and jealousy could turn her into a fury. Poor Princess Labukhin was punished for her beauty at the Empress's order: her tongue was cut off, she received twenty strokes of the knout on her bare body, and was sent to Siberia.

The Grand Duke was not cruel, but his intellectual interests were no greater than his aunt's. With the years his craving for drink increased so much that his sober moments became rare. In his drunken fury he would smash things and treat his wife as no woman, let alone a princess, should be treated. Yet he recognised her mental superiority and would call her, jokingly, "Madame la Ressource", a woman who knows her way around.

Catherine had come into this life as the merest child. Her education, as we have seen, had been incomplete; she had no one to advise her and had to rely on her own resources. Certainly she was not the woman to lead a life of chaste retirement in the midst of a frivolous court: her temperament would have forbidden it. But she did not allow her sensuality to master her. Her limitless ambition sustained her, and the thought of the part she was one day going to play in public life—even at Peter's side. She realised that Fate had thrown her together with this weakling, but that their life together was merely accidental; and her personal ambition no less than her deep-rooted craving for enlightenment drove her on and prescribed her path. With admirable energy she therefore worked to become accomplished and well-read, the more so as she could see that Russian society had not as yet achieved even a veneer of European civilization.

Being young and without a spiritual guide during the first few years of her bleak married life, she concentrated on novels—and not always the best. The most popular authors of her day were Madame Scudéri and La Calprenède, both of whom wrote chiefly lascivious stories in which sensuality and vice predominated. Those books may have given her ideas. The first really valuable book she read were the letters of Madame de Sévigné. Catherine devoured them and later became an apt disciple of this witty letter-writer. The Empress's letters to Voltaire, Grimm, Diderot show clearly what a great character she was to become. Her correspondence fills whole volumes.

After reading Sévigné she discovered Voltaire and became his receptive and ardent disciple. Above Montesquieu, above Tacitus, Plato and many other great writers, Voltaire remained her master, her idol and her oracle. Her adoration for the Philosopher of Ferney was boundless, and she studied all his writings with singular zeal. Though not particularly effusive otherwise, she used terms of fervent admiration whenever she mentioned in later years the man who had formed her intellectual life, and whom she was never to meet. To Grimm, who praised her style, she wrote: "If there is really some power, depth and grace in my letters and my expressions I owe it all to Voltaire; for long have we been reading, studying and re-reading everything that dropped from his pen. I may well claim to have attained so delicate a sense of his style that I have never been in doubt as to whether something was written by him or not. The lion's claw strikes in a way not yet imitated by any man." In following her great example, Catherine gradually became one of the greatest and least inhibited realists ever to have sat on a throne. Ever more intense became her study of works on philosophy, history and political economy, as though she wanted to prepare herself for her future rule. At that period of her development she kept a kind of diary—jottings that already display the optimistic conception of the world to which she was to remain faithful to the end. In these leaves of her diary we also find her first attempts to deal with problems and her own conceptions of law, legislation and other fundamentals of government.

Yet side by side with such serious-minded studies she found time to interest herself in Brantôme's "Vie des dames galantes". There is reason to believe that Catherine was greatly influenced by his lascivious descriptions, and made Queen Johanna II of Naples her ideal. King Henry IV of France may have been another of her examples, not only as a popular ruler but also because of his many amorous adventures. In time she proved able to surpass him in the number of her amours: Henry's mistresses were fewer than Catherine's lovers.

Meanwhile her married life continued in complete monotony, while Peter's company became ever more insufferable. Fortunately he devoted a great deal of his time to his various love affairs, or would spend hours on end at masquerades or in drinking bouts. From time to time, in moments of surfeit, he would come back to Catherine and entertain her with his latest adventures or crazy notions; or he would play the violin for her, walking from one room to the other while producing horrible screechings. During an entire winter he plagued his wife with an idea of his: he was going to build a pleasure palace near Oranienbaum that was to look like a Capuchin monastery. All inmates were to wear monkish habit to gratify his fondness of fancy dress. To please him, Catherine would draft a hundred plans for the palace, and he would change them a hundred times. That palace was never built.

But these were not the worst of her sufferings. Peter, in order to overcome the boredom of Oranienbaum, had bought ten huge hunting dogs, of which the Empress, his aunt, must not know. The hounds spent the whole day in the Grand-Ducal living rooms and at night shared the marital chamber, where they not only spread a pestilential stench but troubled the Duchess's sleep with their barking and panting, whilst her spouse snored at her side, heavy with drink. There were other nights when Peter would amuse himself like a child and play with dolls and other toys. A quantity of them was spread over the bed after he and Catherine had retired for the night. Sometimes Catherine would play with him and laugh at his foolish conceits. It happened that Madame Choglokov knocked at the door and almost surprised them: then she had to be kept away until all the toys were hurriedly hidden under the bedclothes. When the governess entered, she would inform them of Her Majesty's great displeasure that Their Imperial Highnesses were not asleep yet. When she had gone, the toys were brought up again with much hilarity, and the Grand Duke would play with them till he fell asleep in the early hours. Next to dolls, puppet shows gave him endless amusement. The shows he gave had to be attended by his entire entourage, including the Duchess and his mistresses. At other times he would train his dogs, cruelly ill-treating them; or he would put all his servants into uniform and hold some idiotic court-martial. When Catherine one day entered one of the two rooms they shared at Oranienbaum she found Peter in full dress uniform, booted and spurred, his officers and servants surrounding him in solemn silence. Catherine expected some court ceremonial that she did not know, but what was taking place was merely the military execution of—a rat. The poor beast had eaten one of the papier-maché sentries guarding the toy castle Peter loved to play with; he had formed a special court-martial from among his officers and servants which duly condemned the rat to death by hanging—and there it dangled in the middle of the room!

Every day this Czar-to-be invented some new trick of the kind. All this took place in the Grand Duchess's inner apartments, for the Empress must not know. Nor did he lack cunning. One day he invited Catherine with all her ladies to his room, to have a lovely surprise. His gentlemen were already with him. One after the other had to climb on a chair standing against a wall. High up, the Grand Duke had drilled a hole through the boards and ordered everybody to peep through. The 'Peeping Toms' were not a little surprised to look into a small room where Empress Elizabeth was having a rather intimate little party with a small number of friends, a sight usually restricted to those taking part. Both the Empress and her current favourite were very lightly clad. From this experience Catherine drew a lesson which, if not highly moral, may be called practical: so to conduct her future life that she and her lovers could not be spied upon through peep-holes.

Yet during all the years Catherine devoted to her spiritual development, her youth and hot blood prevented her from becoming a bookworm. She did not lack the high

PETRUS III. IMPERATOR
OMNIUM ROSSIARUM

PETER III

spirits of youth and a taste for fun. Healthy-minded and
well-balanced, she was not stricken with grief at her un-
satisfactory married life. She liked merry company and
enjoyed herself when she could. Her generous nature combined amusement and earnestness, work and enjoyment
without clashing. She knew how to enjoy the fleeting moment, and in the depths of the countryside could become a
child, too, but differently from the Grand Duke. Her games
were childlike, but not childish. She loved blind man's buff
and even as an old woman would join her grand-children
in that game. Or the Grand Duchess would race her ladies,
who were as young as she, proving always the fleetest and
nimblest of them all. She adored dancing and never missed
a dance. She found her greatest pleasure in horse-riding,
which she took up soon after she arrived in Russia and
practised with enthusiasm. She preferred to ride astride,
to which the Empress objected, believing that this might
be the reason why she had no children. So the young
Duchess resorted to a trick: she ordered a saddle that could
be used either way. She wore sensible riding clothes of
durable material, mostly trouser-skirts to enable her to ride
astride. With the Empress at her side, Catherine would
demurely perch on a side-saddle, but the moment she was
alone she jumped down, had the groom alter her saddle
and a few moments later galloped away like an exultant
amazon. No chase was too wild for her; if the horse bolted
and she was thrown she would run after the animal and
bring it back. At Oranienbaum she would often get up at
three in the morning, put on man's clothes, shoulder a
musket and, accompanied only by a footman and an old
huntsman, stalk among the reeds to shoot ducks. She was
independent in everything, however meek and obedient she
appeared to those in authority over her; her soul was un-
trammelled, unconfined, masterful and superior to anyone

at court. Befor ther lay a bountiful future, sensual delight, glory and splendour—full satisfaction for her queenly instincts. But still she had to wait, to restrain herself and— to obey.

CHAPTER IV

The First Lapse

LIFE AT A COURT WHERE the atmosphere was charged with
eroticism and amorous intrigues were commonplace, could
not fail to have its effects on a woman like Catherine. Early
in life she had learned to dissemble, to resort to subterfuge
in order to elude her watchers. Though hating lies, she
often had to use evasion, and this in time spoiled her naturally straightforward character. Every man at court soon
noticed that the Grand Duchess's relations with her husband were indifferent and cool, and that Peter cared not
at all for his charming spouse. She, on the other hand, was
eminently desirable, and therefore exposed to temptation.
Nearly every man who came into her orbit fell in love with
her—even though it was not always the idealistic kind of
love. Even her governor, whom Elizabeth had believed to
be proof against all temptation, succumbed to a passionate
attachment for his graceful young charge. Choglokov had
been cold and distant at first, but soon he began to weary
Catherine with declarations of love, writing poetry for her
and emitting amorous sighs—but all in vain. Catherine,
though not particularly fastidious, preferred her males
handsome, and therefore rejected Choglokov's love because
he was ugly and stupid, and not for moral reasons.

Young and handsome Count Cyril Razumovsky, a younger
brother of Elizabeth's favourite, would certainly have been
more successful with the Grand Duchess, if he had been

bolder. But he worshipped at a distance. He was content to look at her. Catherine met him in 1749 at Rajova, near Moscow, where the Choglokovs had their country estate. She had to spend an entire summer there, while the Empress Elizabeth performed her devotions in nearby Troitza Convent. Catherine would have been bored to death with the dull Choglokovs, if some gay young blades from among the country nobility had not helped her to while away the time. Among them was Count Razumovsky. Though his large estate, where he kept a splendid open house, lay on the other side of Moscow, he would travel forty or fifty versts by coach or on horseback every day to visit the Choglokovs while Catherine was staying with them. He was very gay and with his witty quips greatly amused Catherine, who loved merriment above all. Razumovsky was, however, very restrained, especially in his manner towards Catherine, whom he courted so unobtrusively that she completely failed to notice that his daily visits were meant for her alone. It was only twenty years later that she thought of asking Razumovsky what had induced him to make those long trips to Rajova. "Love", replied Razumovsky. "Love?", asked Catherine, "with whom on earth could you have been in love?"—"With you", he retorted drily, causing Catherine to guffaw at her own lack of perception.

But there were others around the Grand Duchess who were less inclined to restrain their feelings, and they were neither as ugly nor as inept as Choglokov. They knew how to approach the young Duchess, who was no prude. One of the Chernichevs returned to Court from exile in 1745; this time it was Zachar and not Andrew who lifted his eyes to Catherine—but his name made no difference to her. Zachar saw that during his six years' absence the Grand Duchess had become even more beautiful, more attractive, more desirable, and did not fail to tell her so. Catherine, always susceptible to flattery, discovered that this gallant officer, too, had grown more attractive, and a flirtation began. At a masked ball where people exchanged little mottoes, couched in poetical language, Zachar Chernichev slipped into the Grand Duchess's hand a note that contained an ardent confession of love. Catherine, amused by this game, replied to Zachar's sentiments in equally passionate language. Encouraged by his rapid success, he whispered into her ear as they danced: he had a thousand things to tell her, but could do so only if they were alone—in her room. He was going to visit her late that night, disguised as a lackey. Catherine did not rebuke him for his boldness, nor did she reject his suggestion, but merely pointed out the danger. History does not tell us whether Zachar Chernichev saw all his desires fulfilled that night; what is certain is that later he had no need to disguise himself in order to meet his beloved. There are in existence letters addressed to him by the Grand Duchess which, though originally published anonymously, are undoubtedly genuine; they leave no doubt that Zachar's relations with her were more than a flirtation. Early in 1752, however, he had to return to his regiment, abandoning Catherine to her solitude. But Sergei Saltikov was soon to console her for this separation.

He, too, belonged to her entourage. He was her chamberlain, and he was less shallow than most other men at Court. "He was as beautiful as the day," Catharine says of him. No one was more handsome, more noble than he at the Empress's Court or at Catharine's. An accomplished courtier, Sergei knew how to hide his failings. Catherine does not entirely absolve him of a certain bent for intrigue, and lack of principles; yet he pleased her despite these faults —or perhaps because of them. When she met him he was twenty-six years of age and had been married for two years to one of the Empress's maids-of-honour, Matrena Pavlovna. It had been a love match, but Sergei was no paragon of fidelity and led a gay life. In Petersburg, where triangular love affairs were the order of the day, he endangered the peace of many a young married couple. His success with women emboldened Saltikov to lift his eyes to the Grand Duke's spouse, especially as she was known to have a weakness for men of his kind. Yet Saltikov was more cunning than his predecessors. He courted Catherine so delicately, yet so markedly, that she could not fail to believe his attentions to be prompted by genuine tenderness and sincere affection rather than by the vanity that must have led him to sue for her favours. Every day throughout the summer he displayed the greatest attentiveness: he had eyes only for her, listened eagerly to the least of her words, and she had only to express a wish to have it fulfilled. Knowing Catherine's delight in amusement, fun and games, he realised that she was going to be grateful to anyone who would enliven the monotony of Oranienbaum. He was good company and every day invented something new to entertain his adored Grand Duchess. As he had much influence with Peter he easily induced him to give splendid galas, organise hunting parties or excursions whose centre was always Catharine. She was grateful to the young courtier, her eyes, her smile promising a world of bliss. With every day she appeared more beautiful, more alluring. He told her so, and she was delighted to hear him. In the end Saltikov was over head and ears in love with the charming Grand Duchess whose healthy, though sometimes coarse, gaiety, whose wit and pleasant humour captivated all those near her. He, too, pleased Catherine; but she wanted to be conquered. In later years the Empress had to take the first step, but at that time no throne prevented her from being all woman.

Saltikov was not long to begin a siege of whose outcome

after him; but he turned round and cheerily called back: "Yes, yes!"—And he was right.

While the Grand-Ducal court was at Oranienbaum, Empress Elizabeth most of the time resided in Petersburg. When important court functions occurred, Peter and Catherine would come to the Capital in order to take part. In Petersburg it was easier for Catherine to evade the spying glances of her retinue. She had only to pretend some slight indisposition in order to be excused appearance at the theatre, dances and other festivities. And thus it happened that one such night in Petersburg made Saltikov the happiest of men. She stayed alone in her room. The Grand Duke, much too obtuse to notice his chamberlain's interest in his wife, and himself at that time in love with one of his Grand Duchess's ladies, Marfa Isayevna Shaffirova, furthered their meetings. Repeatedly he asked Saltikov to leave some gay party and keep the ailing Duchess company. Neither Catherine nor her lover quarrelled with such solicitude. But one day even unsuspecting Peter became uneasy and said: "Sergei Saltikov and my wife are deceiving Choglokov: they make him dance to their tune and laugh at him into the bargain." But he did nothing, obviously indifferent to his wife's doings.

Though Saltikov had promised Catherine that their love would remain a secret he was by no means cautious in his visits, and soon the Empress heard of them. She was, however, much angrier with the Choglokovs who had allowed themselves to be fooled, than with Saltikov. More as a matter of form he was banished from Court for one month, together with his friend, Leon Narishkin. It even seemed as though Elizabeth was not displeased that Catherine should have a lover, for she had long since learned all about her nephew's married life. She was concerned for the continuation of the dynasty. Had she been really angry with

Saltikov she would probably have punished him much more harshly, as she had Andrei Chernichev. The fact that she did not seems to indicate that she must have had her reasons.

Saltikov's absence from Court became prolonged, for he fell ill, and only in February, 1753, could he rejoin his mistress. But Catherine's heart was fickle. She had meanwhile formed a small circle of intimates, mostly young men; it was only by way of exception that she enjoyed feminine company. Among these young men there was one whom she liked best because of his high spirits, and who had been near her before—Leon Narishkin, Saltikov's friend, who had been banished from Court together with him. But Narishkin had not fallen ill but returned when his term of banishment was over, and he was just about to triumph over absent Saltikov when Sergei, in the nick of time, returned. Thus Narishkin continued his part as the Grand Duchess's court jester to her death. "He was the quaintest person I ever knew", she says of him, "no one knew better than he how to make me laugh." Narishkin was a born clown, yet not without wit. His clever sallies greatly amused Catherine who always had a keen sense of humour.

Saltikov had become more careful after his return. Less fiery, less daring, he showed his love less openly. Catherine reproached him, for she was by no means cautious; but he did not want to risk a second banishment. One day Chancellor Bestushev received him in private. Mysteriously, he drew him to one side and told him significantly that he was going to remove those stupid Choglokovs from the Grand Duchess's household; instead, he was going to give her gentle Madame Vladislava, who was completely pliable and would never betray a secret to the Empress. Saltikov goggled with amazement: what was Bestushev driving at? It was only when Bestushev concluded the interview with the

remark that the welfare of Empire and Throne were now
in Saltikov's hand that he understood.

Overjoyed, he went to tell the Grand Duchess. She had
been having a similar interview with her governors, at the
Empress's behest. After a lengthy, moralising introduction,
Madame Choglokov intimated that the Duchess must provide an heir to the throne. Since it seemed that the Grand
Duke was incapable of doing the needful, she must sacrifice
herself for her country and defy convention. In the end
she told her quite frankly to choose between Saltikov and
Narishkin. It was probably the latter the Grand Duchess
preferred. "No, no", exclaimed Catherine, not caring whether
she was betraying herself. "In that case it's the other one",
replied the virtuous duenna. "You will see that I shall put
no obstacles in your way."

From now on Catherine could sacrifice herself for her
country without fear or punishment. The gods co-operated
and rewarded Russia with an heir. Finally, after two mis-
carriages, the much-desired prince (later Paul I) was born
on September 20, 1754. Not only Catherine's memoirs but
also the writings of Champeaux and other contemporaries
leave no doubt as to Saltikov's paternity. Nobody at Court
believed Paul to be Peter's son. The Marquis de l'Hôpital
even went to the length of asserting that Elizabeth exchanged a child of her own for Catherine's—undoubtedly
a fable. Catherine herself may be regarded as the only reliable witness, and in her memoirs she states quite openly
that Saltikov was the father of her son.

Historically, the point is unimportant, for before the
world Paul was the Czarevitch, the heir to the throne.
Strangely enough he showed a marked resemblance to
Peter, both in his character and in his ugliness, facts which
might give rise to the belief that Peter was his father after
all. But then, Peter hated the child. At any rate, there was

a prince, not to be argued away. It is strange that the
mother did not show much affection for her child either—
the child of love, according to her own admission. This lack
of maternal affection may find its explanation in the fact
that Catherine hardly saw her son at all in his first few
years. Immediately after his birth the Empress grabbed
the heir to the throne and carried him into her own apartments. In order not to miss him for a moment she nursed
him herself. Conditions were in every way unnatural for
Catherine. Of her, his mother, little notice was taken; she
had done her duty. She was left alone with one woman who,
completely ignorant of what had to be done, dared not apply
the treatment required, whilst the midwife had disappeared
with the Empress and the new-born child. The Grand Duke
appeared at her bedside for a brief moment but left at once
and noisily celebrated the happy event in an adjoining room
with his cronies and many bottles of Champagne.

Thus, in a worse plight than the lowliest peasant woman,
the Grand Duchess lay on her bed of pain, devoid of all
care. It was three hours later that Countess Shuvalov, in
full court dress, came to Catherine's bedside and gave her
some attention. Neither on that day nor on the next did
anyone but the Countess enter Catherine's room. It was as
though she had ceased to exist. Everything turned around
the small being she had brought into the world: it embodied all hopes and expectations. Three days after the
child had been baptised Elizabeth, as if to pay her for her
trouble, sent her a golden platter with 100,000 roubles and
some jewelry. The diamonds were of moderate size, but the
money pleased Catherine, for as always she was in debt.
But she was not to enjoy the gift for long: a few days later
Cherkassov, the Empress's secretary, called upon the Grand
Duchess and urged her to return the money—for the time
being. Her Majesty had issued another *ukase* to the same

amount, but unfortunately there was not a single copeck in hand at the moment. Peter was jealous of Catherine's 100,000 roubles; as the Czarevitch's father he felt himself entitled to the same present. Elizabeth could not refuse, and thus Catherine had to give way.

A fortnight after her son's birth the Grand Duchess was informed that Saltikov had been sent away from Court. Elizabeth entrusted him with the hanourable mission of informing the Court of Sweden of the Czarevitch's birth, but this was by way of punishment rather than reward. He did not come back. When, having accomplished his mission, he was about to return to Petersburg, the Empress sent a courier to order him to proceed to Hamburg, as Russian Minister. It was obvious that he was being banished from his beloved.

Catherine suffered under this separation. Her former gaiety gave way to melancholy; she felt lonely. Maternity brought her no happiness: she had been but a vessel to carry the future Czar. Anybody might have been the child's father—Andrei or Zachar Chernichev, Leon Narishkin, Sergei Saltikov, or even Choglokov. Nobody seemed interested. Catherine's mother love was thus smothered in an empty cradle, an unfulfilled, frustrated love, and the frivolity of Court life. And since she was sensual by nature, sensuality drove her into the arms of other men and to new debauches. Her heart no longer played a dominant part, though she never acted quite without consulting her feelings when choosing her lovers.

For some time handsome Saltikov still retained her affection. She often wrote to him and had letters from him. Loneliness and distance even seemed to enhance her passion for him; but it was not in her to remain faithful. A handsome stranger whom chance had brought to Russia made her forget her lover. And, for the first time in her life, her love went hand in hand with politics.

CHAPTER V

Stanislas Poniatovsky

CATHERINE DID NOT NEGLECT herself before she met the man who, for the first time, possessed not only her body but also her heart. She worked assiduously, developing her own personality and establishing her position in Russia. Not for a moment did she cease to think of the throne. Her clear discernment lent her more foresight than might have been expected of so young a woman. She became a personage and a power to be reckoned with. She had managed very cleverly to gain influential allies both at Court and abroad, and men like Bestushev, originally her enemy, were convinced that Catherine and not Peter was to reign one day. The Prussian Ambassador, Mardefeld, told her to her face that she was going to hold the reins, and many people around her shared that view. Foreign powers did not remain ignorant of the part for which the Grand Duchess was preparing herself and realised that she represented the only strong personality at Court. Since Elizabeth's health was known to be indifferent owing to her increasingly irregular mode of life, the Grand Duchess was considered the pivotal point of the Russian Court. Peter no longer counted and made no effort to gain influence.

By establishing her own position, by guarding her interests and devoting herself to the study of science and literature, Catherine sought to establish her mental balance which, failing these pursuits, would have been irretrievably destroyed in the maelstrom of her passions. After the birth of the Czarevitch her physical condition exacted greater quiet and solitude. Saltikov was no longer there, and most of the people around her failed to appeal to her mind. The Grand Duke meant nothing to her; she grew further apart from him and went her own way. Petere, who changed his mistresses more frequently than Catherine did her lovers, was in any case absorbed in another infatuation. This time it was the young Countess Elizabeth Voronzov, the sister of that Princess Dashkov who was to prove fatal to Peter. Catherine, for reasons of policy and expediency, at that time formed friendly relations with the Shuvalovs, the Empress's intimates, and the Razumovskys. They formed a faction which opposed Peter's succession after Elizabeth's death and wanted to proclaim a regency, with little Paul as Czar. Catherine realised that it was better to be on good terms with these circles.

At that time she lived with her books. Once again, and with deeper understanding, she read Montesquieu's "De l'esprit des Lois", drawing many a good lesson from a book that was to become the basis of her own legislation. She once remarked that Montesquieu's work ought to be the breviary of every reasonable monarch, and she did in fact take it as her guide. She had now become an ardent disciple of Voltaire. Later, she was to absorb some of the ideas of Diderot, d'Alembert, Grimm and others as well; but at this juncture she was entirely devoted to the great Free Thinker with whom she kept up a most interesting and amiable correspondence. It is surprising that somebody as cultured as Catherine should have loved neither poetry nor music. Though she would listen politely to the verses of Ségur and others, she never perceived their beauties. Similarly, music, even by the greatest masters, left her completely unmoved. She only went to a concert when she had to put in an appearance, and in the theatre ordered the music to stop in the interval. The only kind of music that appealed to her was dance music—because it served a purpose.

Her ambition grew with the years. She had now been in Russia for ten years, had almost completely mastered the language, and daily observed and adopted local customs. Her entourage, with a few exceptions, consisted only of Russians. Her predilection for Russians extended to her lovers: only Poniatovsky and later Zoritch were foreigners, and since one was a Pole and the other a Serb, they were at any rate Slavs. She became a complete Russian. As though foreseeing her destiny, she prepared herself, all alone, for the great part she was one day to play.

Foreign diplomats had so high an opinion of the Grand Duchess's intelligence, discernment and knowledge that they would secretly consult her first in difficult political negotiations, as she surpassed all the Empress's ministers. She often managed to get her views and advice accepted by the Czarina and her advisers who did not notice that they were following Catherine's lead. But the more of a power she became, the greater grew the tension between herself and Elizabeth, who possessed neither Catherine's intelligence and knowledge nor her strength of character. Elizabeth treated her with petty mistrust. Peter had long since lost his aunt's confidence, and angry scenes took place between them. Elizabeth even threatened him with the fate of Peter the Great's son, Alexei; or that she was going to send both him and Catherine back to Germany. It is no exaggeration to say that in the end Peter completely lost any freedom of action he might have had and was treated "like a prisoner of State under open arrest." Elizabeth, too, was not averse to the idea of excluding him from the succession and appointing his son in his stead.

In these circumstances it was natural that the Grand

Duchess should try to establish connections and make friends. While Peter sank deeper and deeper, consorting only with menials and army officers of low rank his wife rose to become the centre of political activity. Eminent foreign diplomatists sought her company, her influence; they felt that the future belonged to her alone.

In 1755, Sir Charles Hanbury Williams was sent to Elizabeth's Court as British Ambassador; he was to counteract the rapprochement between Russia and France. He was accompanied by his secretary, a young Pole by the name of Count Stanislas Poniatovsky. He was a handsome and elegant young man, witty, gay, a brilliant squire of dames and thus very much at home at a court where amusements and festivities seemed to predominate. This was realised by correct and somewhat stiff Sir Charles who was naturally concerned with the success of his mission. He was to renew the treaty of subsidy concluded with Elizabeth in 1742 and make sure of a contingent of Russian troops in the event of war with France. But it was difficult to conduct serious conversations with pleasure-loving Elizabeth. She went from one masquerade, one ball to another, while her frequent banquets left her half-intoxicated. Williams realised that serious political negotiations with this luxurious and indolent Empress were out of the question: he must look elsewhere. His diplomatic intuition soon told him that Catherine and not Peter was the dominant personality at the 'small' court, and he therefore began to frequent the Grand Ducal court. He was always accompanied by young Poniatovsky whom he had met in Dresden, at the court of the King of Poland and Saxony; he took him along on all his travels in order to prepare him for a diplomatic career.

At that time Poniatovsky was twenty-two years old. Though he did not possess Saltikov's beauty he had other attractions, among them the cultured refinement so easily

acquired by Poles in France. He had for some time formed
part of that brilliant and cultured Paris society whose spell
influenced all Europe. He was one of those youngsters Voltaire liked to describe in his novels, a "bel esprit" with all
the advantages and failings implied by that term. He knew
how to display his talents and capabilities to the best advantage and in addition was most charming and discreet.
He had all the enthusiasm, the idealism and sentimentality
of youth, though he was by no means unselfish. On the
contrary, he never overlooked his own advantage. Catherine,
sharing all his attributes with the exception of sentimentality, was bound to be attracted by the young man. All the
men she knew had come to her with many amorous adventures and a stormy past behind them; but Stanislas was said
to have no past, despite the fact that he had spent some
time in Paris. Yet he did not act the innocent. Even though
inexperienced in love he knew court life and—possibly by
instinct—women; for it is not always the libertine who
really understands women. Poniatovsky was enchanted by
Catherine, who had blossomed into a beauty. He has left
us a description of her which, though perhaps seen with the
eye of love, shows how greatly the Duchess's beauty must
have impressed him. She was then twenty-five years old.

"At that time", he writes, "her beauty had reached that
point which is usually for every woman the highest she
attains. With her black hair, she had a dazzling whiteness
of skin, a vivid colouring, large blue eyes, black and long
eyebrows, a Grecian nose, a mouth that looked made for
kissing, perfect hands and arms, a slight figure, tall rather
than short, a carriage that was lively yet full of nobility, a
pleasing voice, and a laugh as merry as the humour which
enjoyed the most playful and childish amusements."

Yet Poniatovsky, though not timid by nature and in this
case rather enterprising, hesitated some time before ap-

proaching the Grand Duchess. He had heard too much of the cruel fate reserved for men who had enjoyed the favours of beautiful princesses, especially in Russia. He saw the spectre of Siberia where so many were left to languish, once they had ceased to please their mistresses.

However, an intermediary soon appeared in the person of Bestushev. He would rather see a foreigner close to the Grand Duchess than the Russian, Saltikov, who had after all returned to Petersburg. Bestushev established the first contact, using that obliging fellow, Leon Narishkin, as go-between. He soon convinced the young Pole that Catherine was no Messalina, no Mary Stuart, no Christine of Sweden. She was not, like the Empresses Catherine I and Elizabeth, going to banish her lovers to Siberia, once they had done their duty and ceased to please. Poniatovsky liked nothing better than to establish closer relations with the Grand Duchess; but first he must defeat Saltikov. But Saltikov's ardour was fading; he was no longer the same fiery lover. Other arms, other eyes, other lips caused him to shorten the hours he spent with the Grand Duchess, until one night Catherine waited for him until three in the morning—in vain.

Poniatovsky, the gallant knight, would never have kept a beautiful woman waiting. One day he was honoured with an engaging look, an amiable smile, some pleasant words. Now he must grasp his chance with both hands, or forever hold his peace. He took his chance, and soon it was no secret at court that he was the chosen one. He became one of Catherine's familiar circle. At that time Count Horn was the Swedish Ambassador in Petersburg. He was one of Poniatovsky's intimates and was admitted to the Grand Duchess's inner circle of friends. As he entered Catherine's salon one day her little lap-dog rushed at him, barking, and bit him in the leg. It did the same to every one who came in; but when Poniatovsky entered, the little dog did not bark but wagged its tail. Horn, a good observer, said smilingly to Poniatovsky: "My friend, there is nothing more danger-our than a lap-dog. The first thing I used to give to the women I loved was such a dog: from its behaviour I would learn whether there was someone in greater favour than myself."

The British Ambassador thus gained a useful supporter, for Poniatovsky's influence over Catherine increased. But Williams also employed another means of persuasion—gold, to whose glitter even Grand Duchesses are susceptible. All her life Catherine required immense sums for her personal expenditure; the fantastic treasures of her realm proved hardly adequate in later years. Elizabeth kept the Grand Duchess relatively short, and she was always in debt. She convinced the Ambassador that in order to be useful to him she must have cash in hand; she did not mind bribing the Empress's chambermaids. In this manner some 44,000 roubles of English money came into Catherine's hands. She even gave a receipt for this amount and pledged her word of honour to repay it later. In 1764 she actually ordered her Minister, Panin, to settle the matter with Buckingham, the British Ambassador, but England delicately overlooked this little item.

Soon Catherine was under the influence of the trio, Wil-liams, Bestushev and Poniatovsky, the latter, of course, carrying the greatest weight with her. Love and politics, that forbidden field, went together. Yet despite everything Williams's mission failed, and he had to leave Russia in 1759. In a letter dated August 19, 1759, Catherine gave him her word that she would do everything in her power to further the Anglo-Russian alliance. She was always going to remember her personal indebtedness to the King and, she added significantly in conclusion, her dearest wish was to see Williams triumphantly return to Russia. In this manner her secret intelligence with various politicians exposed her to great danger. What she did not do, Bestushev or Poniatovsky did: all three were working in concert.

The Court soon noted the young Pole's influence over Catherine. Elizabeth was little concerned with the Grand Duchess's morals: she judged the behaviour of others no more severely than her own; but she was easily influenced by those around her. One day Poniatovsky was ordered to leave Russia at once. But in Bestushev Catherine had gained a powerful friend. He gave her back her lover, for Bestushev's influence with Elizabeth was still decisive. After a mere three months' absence Stanislas appeared again at the Court of Russia, this time invested with a dignity that lent him both authority and influence. He returned as the Envoy of King Augustus III of Poland, his breast adorned with the Order of the White Eagle. This, too, was Bestushev's work. He needed Poniatovsky as much as Catherine. Through his friend, Count Brühl, the First Minister of the King of Poland and Elector of Saxony, he had easily obtained this favour for his protégé.

Once again gold came into play. Brühl knew that the Grand Duchess and her husband were chronically short of money, since Elizabeth preferred to waste her wealth on her favourites and in sumptuous feasts. He therefore handed 6,000 ducats to the young Ambassador who was gradually to lend them to the Grand Duke, as the occasion offered, in order to gain his friendship as well. Poniatovsky liked nothing better, for to have an enemy in the Grand Duke might have become dangerous. In this, he did not forget his own interest, for while being in love he had not ceased to be ambitious. A man of his intelligence and talents did not find things difficult at the Court of Russia. Elizabeth would spend hours on her knees before her ikons, or

else with her finery or at court fêtes. Going from one extreme to another, she indulged to excess, now her debauchery, now her bigotry. After such debauches she had to be
carried to bed in a drunken stupor. She did not suffer anyone to undress her: her maids would cut her clothes open
or put her to bed as she was. As a consequence of her irregular way of life she had frequent convulsions and other
ailments. More than ever, Catherine's party anticipated a
new reign, and there arose a kind of conspiracy, led by
Chancellor Bestushev. Through Poniatovsky he sent Catherine a manifesto in which he outlined his intentions
in the event of the Empress's death. Grand Duke Paul
was to be proclaimed Czar, and Catherine was to take
part in the regency. For himself, Bestushev claimed the
rank of Lieutenant-General in charge of four Guards regiments, and the presidency of the three Imperial Colleges,
for Foreign Affairs, War, and Admiralty. Catherine did
not object to this plan and, through her lover, conveyed
to Bestushev her thanks for his good intentions. She merely
added that she thought them difficult to carry out. Six
months prior to this, in August, 1757, she, together with
Bestushev, had caused General Apraxin to retreat after
the successful battle of Gross-Jägerndorf, because she
might have required part of the army in the event of the
Empress's death. In short, she grew ever bolder in her
political designs, and she very nearly fell into the abyss of
intrigue. Fortunately, only Bestushev fell victim to the
thunderbolt of the Empress's wrath when she learned of
this treasonable project. Vice-Chancellor Voronzov, the
uncle of Peter's mistress, denounced him to the Empress
who, in February, 1758, had him arrested and sent to
Siberia.

Catherine learned of Bestushev's arrest through a letter
sent to her by Poniatovsky. She was thunderstruck, but

had sufficient presense of mind to burn all compromising papers and appear in public as if ignorant of the whole affair. In this dangerous crisis she displayed a remarkable fortitude which enabled her to overcome all difficulties. Elizabeth had no real proof against her and had to confine the expression of her disfavour to a few week's exclusion from her presence.

These hours of worry were soon over, and Catherine's cheerfulness carried the day. Poniatovsky increasingly dominated her heart and her senses, spending day and night with her. She could no longer live without him. Peter was now keeping Countess Voronzov, Madame Treplov and a young German dancer, and was thus fully occupied. The Grand Duchess could do what she liked in her own apartments. Leon Narishkin also arranged occasional meetings at the house of his sister-in-law where she could be with Poniatovsky. Catherine loved escapades of this kind, especially when she could disguise herself in male attire.

One day, however, the Grand Duke had an idea that something else besides love might occasion those nightly trysts between Catherine and Poniatovsky. He feared for his life. One night in July, 1758, towards dawn, Poniatovsky, in disguise, was leaving the Grand Duchess's apartments, when suddenly a patrol of Peter's soldiers pounced upon him, arrested him and led him before the Grand Duke. Peter wanted to know whether his suspicions of Catherine were true, and whether their meetings were prompted by something other than tender dalliance. Poniatovsky returned adroit answers that did not compromise anybody, and Peter had no choice but to release him. Yet Poniatovsky might have paid dearly for his carelessness. Peter's mistrust, at any rate, still persisted, and therefore the clever Pole tried by all means to win the Grand Duke's friendship. How better to achieve this than through the

Duke's influential mistress. Elizabeth Voronzov was a conceited woman who would have liked to play the Pompadour whilst lacking her intelligence. Neither was Peter a Louis XIV. However, the Countess felt immensely flattered when in a position to grant minor favours. The astute diplomat approached her. "How easy for you, Countess, to make certain people happy!", he whispered into her ear as he danced with her at a court ball. The Countess was only too happy to appear in the role of Lady Bountiful. That very night she talked to Peter about Poniatovsky and led, or rather dragged, the latter into the Grand Duke's room.

Peter, fundamentally good-natured and somewhat stupid, received him with these conciliatory words: "What a fool you were not to take me into your confidence in time!" He then explained that he was by no means jealous and did not begrudge him his happiness. The sentries around Oranienbaum had been posted merely in order to assure his personal safety. From now on Poniatovsky could enter and leave at will; he was going to issue orders to this effect. He was greatly flattered when Poniatovsky shrewdly congratulated him on the efficiency of his soldiers. Peter was happy, and exclaimed: "Now that we are good friends, there's someone wanting", and, as Poniatovsky tells us, "hastened to Catherine's bedroom, pulled her out of bed, giving her no time to put on her stockings and shoes or even a robe, and brought her in in her night attire, exclaiming: 'Well, here he is! I hope you are all pleased with me'." He told his new friend: "Stay to supper with me; you know, I have a mistress, too." The four of them thereupon remained together in jolly company, feasting and joking till four o'clock in the morning, when they separated. This went on for many weeks. Each night Poniatovsky came to see his beloved at Oranienbaum. He used a secret staircase. In her apartments he would find the Grand Duke with

Countess Voronzov, who smoked and drank with him. The company had supper together, and when it was over the Grand Duke would leave with his mistress, exclaiming laughingly: "Good night, children, you don't need me any more." And Stanislas stayed with Catherine.

Catherine was no longer fenced in and guarded from all sides. She had managed to turn even her watchers into friends. She captivated everyone who came near her, attracting the men with her sensuality or her intellect while conquering the women through her boundless kindness and charming manner. Yet there was also something in her that inspired respect, reverence and perhaps even fear. The Chevalier d'Eon says of her: "The Grand Duchess is romantic, bold, passionate. She has brilliant eyes, a fascinating, piercing glance almost like that of some wild creature. Her brow is high ... she is amiable and obliging, but if she draws near me I instinctively fall back a step—she inspires fear."

Catherine undoubtedly fascinated everyone. She even had some influence with Peter. Realising her capability, he had entrusted her with the management of his affairs in Holstein, but ever since Bestushev's arrest she had been deprived of this part of her husband's political duties. Peter was given to understand that the Empress disliked Catherine's interference in these matters; and since he was weak and timid he gave way. Nevertheless he needed Catherine's advice and often came to ask "Madame la Ressource" for it. Otherwise, however, he had not much use for her company: it was not the woman in her but her superior strength of mind that impressed him. Yet her company did not improve his own character. His eccentricities and vices increased. He often got so drunk that he could no longer stand; mouthing a flood of obscene language he would molest Catherine—who had to share his bedroom—in a most repulsive manner. His eyes reddened with drink, he would brag to her all night of his 'conquests'—the ugly, deformed Princess of Courland, pock-marked Countess Voronzov, or some other Dulcinea. If Catherine shammed sleep he would roughly elbow her awake or shout until she opened her eyes and listened to him. Yet she did not think of raising some pretext in order to induce her uncouth husband to sleep in a separate room. They even slept in one bed; this was the tradition. Catherine was the Grand Duke's wife and had to preserve appearances. Elizabeth would have opposed this change in marital habits.

The Poniatovsky scandal became a little too much for Elizabeth, little squeamish as she was; but Catherine did as she liked.The Grand Ducal court lived in a higgledy-piggledy disorder impossible anywhere else but in Russia. Towards the end of 1758 the Grand Duches gave birth to a girl, Grand Duchess Anna. It was an open secret that Poniatovsky was her father. The Grand Duke, in his coarse manner, one day jokingly remarked at dinner: "Heaven knows where she gets all those children from: I had no idea that this one was mine." This pretty speech was, of course, promptly reported to the Duchess by Leon Narishkin. Catherine, who was still lying in, laughed and sent him back to the Grand Duke, asserting on oath that Anna was Peter's child. Narishkin was then to take this information to the "Imperial Grand Inquisitor" in order to pacify him. Catherine was referring to Count Alexander Shuvalov, the head of Elizabeth's secret chancellery. In this way Catherine secured her reputation and kept up appearances. Little Anna died in April, 1759, a few months later. When she was born the Grand Duke gave another proof of his eccentricity. Catherine felt the first pains at half-past one in the morning. Peter immediately put on his full-dress Holstein uniform, complete with riding-boots, spurs, belt and a huge cavalry sabre, and came to Catherine's bedside. When she asked him what this meant he replied—swaying and reeling with drink—that it was on occasions such as this that people recognised their real friends. He had put on the dress proper for the fulfilment of his oath as an officer of Holstein, to defend the Grand Ducal house against all enemies; believing his wife to be alone he had rushed to her defence.

When Catherine had recovered she resumed her wild life. The nights were no longer enough; the days, too, were filled with riotous amusement. She had grown so bold that she no longer feared the Empress. Her personal and political following increased daily. She even managed to bring Elizabeth's lovers and minions over to her side. Elizabeth's latest favourite, Ivan Shuvalov, paid marked attention to the coquettish Grand Duchess. Elizabeth had reason to fear Catherine. She seemed to be aware of it, for she said less and less, and ceased to interfere with the 'young' court. Besides, Catherine was unrivalled in ever new tricks to elude her watchers.

Under the pretext of stopping a draught in her room, she arranged screens to form a kind of partition, a small, intimate room next to her large, silk-curtained bed. She equipped this 'secret' room with easy chairs and tables and used it to receive visitors that must not be seen by others. From outside, this arrangement actually looked as if intended to screen the Grand Duchess's bed from air currents, for the window was completely obscured. If anyone asked what was behind the screens, Catherine would say, her close-stool—a reply typical of her. In this secret cubicle she would throw her intimate 'parties'. Count Poniatovsky usually came disguised in a blond periwig; if some attendant stopped him and asked who he was, he would say: "Musician to the Grand Duke", and was allowed to proceed.

Then there would come the inevitable Narishkin, his sister-in-law, Madame Syenyavin, Ismailov and many others inclined to spend some gay hours: the Grand Duchess's little parties were great fun. She was usually in bed but joined the company simply by drawing a curtain and moving a screen. If Count Shuvalov or some other messenger—or rather spy—from the Empress was announced the curtain was closed, the screen replaced, and the visitor would leave the Grand Duchess, fully convinced that he had found her alone. The moment he left, laughing, feasting and general jollity was resumed. Catherine would ring for her servants —curtain and screens being in position, of course—and declare she was hungry enough for four. Huge platters of meat, fruit and other delicacies were served, while the servants gaped at their mistress's Gargantuan appetite and she, in turn, hugely enjoyed their amazement.

Her entourage was, of course, no better than she. Ladies-in-waiting and maids-of-honour learned their lessons from Elizabeth and Catherine and would receive visitors by day —and by night. True, their gallant knights had to pass some obstacles before joining their lady-loves, but they were easy. The apartments of the young maids-of-honour —purely their official title!—were guarded by Madame Schmidt, Mistress-of-the-Robes, or by the Princess of Courland: that is to say, you had to traverse these ladies' rooms before entering those of the maids. Madame Schmidt was far from being a reliable Cerberus: she was constantly plagued by nocturnal colics, having overindulged in the pleasures of the table, and thus rarely to be found in her room. As for the Princess of Courland, a few personal attentions would be sufficient to clear the road.

So much for the morals of the Court of Russia while Poniatovsky was in favour. But the time came when even his tender passion ceased to move Catherine. When he finally had to leave the Court, his intimacy with the Grand Duchess having become too overt, Catherine was not even sorry to see him depart. She loved variety. Poniatovsky did everything in his power to stay near his beloved. He feigned sickness, took to his bed and did not set foot outside his house in the daytime while visiting the Grand Duchess by night. For some time he managed to keep up this pretence towards Elizabeth and her advisers, but in the end his hour came. He was sent back to the Court of Warsaw. He was to return to Russia later, wearing a king's crown that he owed to his former mistress; yet it was to bring him more misfortune than happiness.

* * *

Not without good reason did Catherine once say to the Marquis de l'Hôpital: "I am a woman of unbridled temerity". Throughout her life she adored adventure and did not despise adventurers, if only they were ingenious or clever in approaching her. Stanislas Poniatovsky was forgotten like Andrei and Zachar Chernichev, like Sergei Saltikov and so many others. There were many gaps in her circle now: her meddling in politics and her intrigues with Bestushev and Apraxin had placed her in grave jeopardy. One false step, and she might one day have disappeared from Court, like the all-powerful Chancellor, and been sent, if not to Siberia, back to Germany. But Catherine knew how to safeguard her position. Her acumen and firmness of purpose not only made her position more bearable but helped her to overcome all intrigues. It was she who began to rule at Court. The Marquis de l'Hôpital wrote: "The fear which dominates all minds in this nation afflicted with despotism, causes all the nobility of the Empire and even the Empress's own ladies to support and sustain the Grand Duchess; they plot in her interest. This faction is led by the Empress's favourite and chamberlain, Shuvalov, together with his cousin, Peter Shuvalov. Only Count Voronzov and Monsieur Alzufiev remain loyal to their Monarch; all the others are intimidated, cowardly and mean, excusing their falsity with the respect they profess they owe to the Grand Duchess. They lend themselves to all her wishes and inform her of everything Her Majesty thinks, does or intends."

Peter stood greatly in awe of his wife, and would have liked nothing better than to see her removed from Court. He used every opportunity to complain and carry tales of her to Elizabeth. Yet although the Empress was not over-fond of the Grand Duchess, Catherine always carried the day, be it through tears and submission or by assuming an attitude of haughty pride. Elizabeth was hesitant by nature and always had to work herself up to having a scene. Weeks would pass until she could bring herself to give vent to her pent-up fury. Yet as soon as she stood face to face with Catherine she felt embarrassed and her efforts to find the right words were noticeable. For many weeks following the Bestushev-Apraxin scandal the Grand Duchess was not admitted to her presence. Catherine sent a written explanation and humbly begged to be sent back to her family in Germany. It is, however, very doubtful whether she thought such dismissal possible. Knowing Elizabeth, she knew that the Empress would not take this line if she herself demanded it. Still, the meeting for which she asked Elizabeth was long deferred.

Catherine, however, was much too astute a diplomat not to see that she must as quickly as possible effect a reconciliation with the Empress—at least for appearance's sake. Her confessor advised her to feign a dangerous illness and, being an accomplished actress, she had no difficulty in doing so. Alexander Shuvalov sent for the Court physicians; but the Grand Duchess seemed so weak that spiritual consolation only appeared indicated. Catherine always knew how to exploit Elizabeth's piety. Her confessor and ally came and spent some time alone with her, and then reported to the Empress that sorrow and suffering had so debilitated the Grand Duchess that she was bound to die unless something was done to relieve her mind.

That same night Elizabeth granted her an audience, but in the presence of Peter and Count Alexander Shuvalov. Peter was jubilant when he heard that his wife was dying, and expressed his intention of marrying Countess Voronzov; but he was soon to sing a different tune. Still, the first part of the audience looked like a triumph for him. Catherine prostrated herself before the Empress and begged her for permission to return to Germany, since she no longer had her confidence. Elizabeth was powerless before Catherine's tears and modest dignity. She bade her rise and said: "God is my witness how many tears I shed when you fell gravely ill on coming to Russia. I would not have kept you here, had I not loved you." There was a sparkle in Catherine's eyes: she sensed that she was winning. When Elizabeth further reproached her for her excessive pride and being so stiff-necked that she barely acknowledged salutations at court, Catherine acted the innocent. Demurely, she said that she must no doubt be too stupid to appreciate the honour of having the Empress's glance rest on so unimportant a person as herself. Elizabeth did not take in the sarcasm, but in Catherine's eyes she saw that tigerish look before which so many men had quailed. Instinctively the Empress recoiled a step and walked to another corner of the room, where the Grand Duke told her all sorts of derogatory stories about his wife. But Elizabeth remembered Catherine's look. She dismissed both of them in a hurry and refused to listen to the Grand Duke's complaints. In the end she found her nephew's faults more grievous than Catherine's, so that Peter in his turn asked to be sent back to Germany. But he, too, stayed on, to meet his fate in Russia.

Only the semblance of peace was established between the two Courts. Elizabeth now liked neither Peter nor Catherine, and rarely met them during the last three years of her life. She considered Catherine an intriguer and Peter a simpleton. Yet to the Grand Duchess this formal reconcil- iation with the Empress was a victory, since it averted the principal danger. For the time being, she asked no more. She gained fresh vigour, fresh courage.

Catherine was now in the flower of her womanhood: at twenty-nine, she had blossomed into a beautiful and accom- plished woman. But her voluptuousness, too, had developed to a degree that can be a woman's ruin. In the spring of 1759 the fire of her passion blazed up once again.

In the battle of Zorndorf, on August 25, 1758, the Rus- sians had captured Count Schwerin, the aide-de-camp of the King of Prussia, and brought him to Petersburg. He was guarded by two Russian officers, one of whom had gained special distinction at Zorndorf. He was Gregory Orlov. Daring, even reckless and brutal, yet endowed with the fatalism of the Oriental, he was of giant stature and her- culean strength. To Catherine, he was more beautiful than Poniatovsky, more beautiful than any man at Court. His tall, strong, well-knit body was crowned by beautifully modelled features—the face of an angel and, incidentally, the only thing that was angelic about Orlov. He was Ca- therine's ideal man, and she idolised him because of his strength.

Orlov was one of five brothers, all of them Guards offi- cers. His brother Alexei was his equal in beauty and strength, and even taller than he. Both of them were later to enjoy the favours of that insatiable woman, but Gregory was and remained her chosen lover. He was far from being Catherine's mental equal: he had little intelligence, next to no education and was used to garrison life with its gambling, drinking orgies and debauches with women—all to excess. Pleasure-mad, licentious, a spendthrift though poor, quarrelsome and uncouth, he was a semi-barbarian—a libertine without refinement. He was a descendant of one of the *strelitzi* Peter the Great had spared. For twelve years this man, next to politics, was to possess Catherine's heart—not because he was intelligent, particularly tender, or apt to be her mentor, but simply because he was physically powerful and of inexhaustible virility. He was health and strength, but also coarseness, incarnate.

Before he met Catherine, Orlov set the tongues of Petersburg wagging by becoming the lover of beautiful Princess Kurakin. He was adjutant to Count P. I. Shuvalov, a cousin of Elizabeth's favourite. This Count Shuvalov was Inspector-General of Artillery, a position much coveted by Guards officers. His beautiful mistress, Princess Kurakin, roused even greater envy, and his adjutant, Gregory Orlov, became his rival. His powerful masculinity won this woman, too. But Orlov was the least discreet of men: soon not only the Court but the whole of Petersburg were discussing this affair. Its most intimate details were bandied about in the Guards barracks. Fortunately for Orlov, Shuvalov died; otherwise he would not have stood for this insult from his subordinate. The affair made Orlov conspicuous, though Catherine would possibly have discovered him without this notoriety, for Orlov was as enterprising as he was handsome. For the first time in her life, however, Catherine now had to take the first step. One of her ladies, Ivanovna Sheregorodskaya, arranged her first rendezvous with Orlov. He grasped the situation at once and realised his chance of making his fortune. The beautiful Princess Kurakin was completely discarded, for the Grand Duchess suffered no other gods beside her.

Catherine, too, was handsome, though she could not vie with the Princess's beauty. But then she was the Grand Duchess, soon, perhaps, to be the Czarina, since Elizabeth's health deteriorated steadily. Orlov realised all this. Catherine, in turn, was also not led by passion alone: her love, too, was influenced by political considerations. Orlov and his four brothers were serving in the four Guards Regiments which were a powerful factor in Petersburg.

Orlov was soon the established and spoilt darling of the Grand Duchess, and made no secret of the fact. As he had divulged his 'secret' affair with Princess Kurakin at the gaming table, over his wine and in the barrack room, so did he now boast of Catherine's favour. Yet it seemed to please her that her love-life was being discussed: her vanity was flattered. Even more remarkable is the fact that meanwhile she continued her intimate correspondence with Poniatovsky and in her letters to her former lover spoke quite openly, and even with a certain boastfulness, of her new love for Orlov. In other letters, many years later, she referred to this period. On one occasion she wrote: "Osten still remembers how Orlov used to follow me everywhere and committed a thousand follies for me. His passion for me was public knowledge."

She enjoyed the company of this healthy brute. She hated all melancholy or sentimentality. Never did she allow sadness to dominate her heart or her surroundings. When she suffered she would hide from everyone for a day or two, have a good cry, but then be precisely as before, cheerful and gay. There were few sad moments in her life. Catherine was naturally sociable and a good companion. Her spirit seemed male rather than feminine, a fact that did not prevent her being desirable as a woman. Her mind and her heart usually went different ways: hardly any of her lovers were her mental equals. Her mind was catered for by her philosophers—Voltaire, d'Alembert, Diderot, Grimm; in conversation with them she would appear so masculine that even these wise men sometimes forgot that they were talking to a woman—and a queen. In one of his talks with her, Diderot—vivacious by nature—so far forgot himself as to slap her knee repeatedly. When, with sudden fright, he became aware of his lack of manners, Catherine said: "Among men anything goes."

Later she had a very few female friends whom she liked for their intellectual powers. About the time that handsome Gregory's star was in the ascendant she became friendly with intelligent, still very youthful Princess Catherine Romanovna Dashkov, as if to make up for the lack of spiritual content in her relations with Gregory and Alexei Orlov. Dashkova, who was to be so useful to her later on when she ascended the throne, was the sister of Peter's paramour, Countess Voronzov, but of an entirely different cast of mind. A third sister was lady-in-waiting to Empress Elizabeth. Young Princess Dashkov was the only woman at the Court of Russia to be the Grand Duchess's mental equal. Catherine met her when Dashkova was only fifteen but lost sight of her for some years and only met her again at the age of eighteen. Apart from this young woman, Catherine at that time was close to her son's tutor, Count Nikita Panin. He had to replace exiled Bestushev as her political adviser. Her party increased every day.

Meanwhile life at Court went on even more wildly, more disorderly than in Poniatovsky's time. The Orlovs, Leon Narishkin and others had unrestricted access to the Grand Duchess's apartments. People there did as they pleased.

Narishkin in particular showed not the least respect for his Mistress's rank. Possibly he knew her too well. One day Catherine found him lying on her couch. When she entered the room he was singing a lascivious song but neither rose nor stopped his singing as he noticed her. Catherine turned on her heel—not indignant or offended, but resolved to play a trick on him. She quickly locked the door so that he could not escape. Then she hastened to her confidante, Leon's sister-in-law, who was always willing to join in any prank started by the Grand Duchess. Both women had bunches of nettles brought in. Armed with them, and accompanied by a maid, they went into the room where Leon, still lying on the couch, was singing his dubious song more loudly than ever. The maid, too, carried a bunch of stinging nettles, and the offender was overpowered by the three of them. They thrashed him so soundly that his face, hands and legs remained covered with bruises and sores for three days. He was unable to appear at Court, so badly did they beat him.

So much for one of the Grand Duchess's less philosophical entertainments.

CHAPTER VI

The Struggle for the Crown

DESPITE HER IRREGULAR and licentious mode of life, Empress Elizabeth was by no means concerned with amusement only; at times she thought about the future of Russia and shuddered at the thought of seeing her country governed after her death by her inept nephew. She had long since recognized Peter's shortcomings, and also the fact that Catherine was no ordinary woman and was going to establish a position of her own. However, she loved neither Peter nor the Grand Duchess. With her favourite, Shuvalov, she often discussed the plan of proclaiming little Grand Duke Paul heir to the throne while exiling his parents; both realised that a weak-minded monarch like Peter would be fatal to his country. But Elizabeth lacked the power of resolution and was hampered by her innate inertia. Perhaps she did not like to think of her death, for she loved life above all. In short, though very fond of the little Grand Duke, she made no change in the succession.

Death overtook the ailing Empress on January 5, 1762. It wrought great changes in the European political situation but caused no upheaval in Russia. Peter III quietly mounted the throne of the Czars without encountering any popular resistance. He remained ignorant of the danger that would have threatened him, had his aunt been more resolute. She even sent for him on the eve of her death, but in that interview touched upon purely personal matters.

She begged him to live in harmony with his wife and always to show love and affection to little Paul. The Grand Duke further had to promise to extend his protection to her two favourites, Alexei Razumovsky and Ivan Shuvalov. Right to the end Elizabeth was thus completely taken up with her private concerns.

Peter and Catherine were at her bedside as she breathed her last. Senator Prince Trubetskoy emerged from the dead Empress's bedroom and proclaimed the new Czar's accession to the Crown.

Peter's first steps as ruling monarch seemed to be guided by surprising reasonableness; but eccentricities of all kinds soon marred this favourable first impression. Peter's greatest fault was trying to Germanize the Russian people; by rejecting everything Russian he caused great offence.

Moreover, he turned his clever wife into his greatest and most dangerous enemy. Frederick the Great is said to have warned him, advising him to make sure of Catherine's friendship; but Peter rejected this good advice. He would have preferred Catharine not to have become Empress at all. She was deliberately passed over on all official occasions; the manifesto issued on the day of Peter's accession mentioned neither her name nor that of the little Grand Duke. No sooner had Peter seized power than he revenged himself, as Catherine's overlord, for the superiority she had displayed while he was yet powerless. He treated her with the greatest lack of attention, depriving her of all influence on the conduct of public affairs and grossly insulting her on many occasions. One day, at the dinner table, he publicly called her *durâ*, the Russian equivalent of "fool". The Czarina had to suffer Peter's mistress occupying the best-appointed apartments in the palace while she herself was housed in a remote wing. Honours were showered on Elizabeth Voronzov, while Catherine had only a small court of loyal followers. At that time she found herself in a gravely critical position, the more so as she was about to give birth to Orlov's child, later the Count Bobrinsky.

Contemporary observers noted her depression, but also the dignity with which she carried herself towards her husband. No complaint passed her lips; tears were her sole defence. The woman "of unbridled temerity" was gone; she now lived in utter seclusion, fortifying herself with her philosophy. In view of Catherine's well-known volatile temperament such behaviour was bound to excite suspicion. Her intimates therefore disbelieved in her seeming meekness and humility, for they knew that she not only despised but hated her husband. She was being treated as a nobody, humiliated by the man whose superior she knew herself to be. So, whilst, bearing humiliation with seeming calmness, she made plan after plan for her deliverance.

If Williams deserves credence, Catherine had told him of her plans in the event of Elizabeth's death five years earlier. She wrote: "I would immediately go to my son's room. If I were to find Alexei Razumovsky there I would leave him with little Paul; if not, I would take the child with me to my room. At the same time I would send a confidential messenger to five Guards officers, [the Orlov brothers]. Each one would put fifty soldiers at my disposal. Then I would send for Bestushev, Apraxin and Lieven. I would go to the room where the Empress had died, and would there accept the Captain of the Guard's oath of loyalty. I would take that officer with me, and if I noticed the least hesitation I would have the Shuvalovs arrested." And she adds, with magnificent daring: "I would not, like Ivan the Terrible, seek refuge with your king, for I am resolved to rule or to perish."

Things turned out somewhat differently from the way outlined in her letter to the British Ambassador; but she came to rule. In the end she gained the upper hand. Peter became ever more attached to Countess Voronzov, and his partisans, Catherine's enemies, endeavoured to strengthen his intention of marrying his mistress. Voronzova was very common: she is reported to have "drunk, smoked and cursed like a soldier, to have dribbled when speaking, being cross-eyed into the bargain." Her behaviour towards the Czarina grew daily more impertinent and insufferable. Already she saw herself as Peter's consort.

It was truly great and noble of Catherine that when she eventually came to power she neither persecuted nor deprived of their liberty those who had tried to do her harm. In this particular case the Empress treated her one-time rival with marked benevolence. When Countess Elizabeth Voronzov had become Princess Palliansky, Catherine appointed her two daughters ladies-in-waiting. Yet this woman had caused her much suffering, even in public. Foreign diplomats were aware of the position: Baron de Breteuil, in a letter of January 15, 1762, reported to the Duke de Choiseul:

"The Empress finds herself in a deplorable position. She is being treated with the greatest public contempt. As I have already remarked, she tries to bear her burden like a philosopher; but I have also told you how little this is compatible with her character. Now I know and no longer doubt that she sustains the Emperor's behaviour and Countess Voronzov's arrogance with great impatience. I am convinced that the Empress, whose courage and impetuosity I know, is one day going to do something out of the ordinary. I know that she has friends who are trying to calm her, but who would risk everything for her, should she demand it."

These friends were: young and daring Princess Catherine Dashkov, Count Nikita Panin, the five Orlov brothers, Leon

Narishkin and his sister-in-law, Madame Sinyavin, Captain Passek, Prince Repnin, Teplov, a Piedmontese named Odard, later Catherine's secretary, and several other persons at court. Princess Dashkov and Count Panin were not only related but also in closest sympathy with each other. They shared the same views and the Princess, whose mind was of almost masculine strength, had tremendous influence on Russia's future Prime Minister. He, she and the brothers Orlov were the chief conspirators against the Czar. They foresaw the danger that threatened Catherine, for they knew that Peter intended to cast off his wife and have her son declared illegitimate. This must be prevented by some quick counter-stroke. Public opinion about the Czar had, however, nothing to do with these purely personal considerations.

The coup d'état that was to cost Peter his throne and later his life was by no means well-prepared and planned in detail. It came about suddenly, and through force of circumstance. There arose a rumour that Peter had already drafted a manifesto announcing the arrest of the Empress and the young Grand Duke; the arrest was to have taken place on the night of July 10/June 29. He intended to solemnise his marriage with Elizabeth Voronzov that same night. A few days before that date he decorated the Countess with the order of St. Catherine. On the morning of July 8/June 27, a rumour spread in Petersburg according to which Catherine had been taken to the fortress of Schlüsselburg. A guardsman called on Captain Passek, one of the conspirators, and informed him that the Empress was in urgent need of help. Another officer who was not in the plot and who had overheard this message arrested Passek on the spot and reported the incident to the Czar, who happened to be at Oranienbaum. The hour of action had come for Catherine and her adherents.

That same night, at five o'clock in the morning of July 9/
June 28, Alxis Orlov walked unannounced into the Empress's bedroom at Peterhof and awakened her. He merely
said: "The time has come." Catherine was drowsy with
sleep and had to collect her thoughts before she understood.
When she asked for further details Orlov told her that
Captain Passek had been arrested, and that she must
hasten to Petersburg to have herself proclaimed sole ruler.
Catherine dressed in great haste and entered a carriage
Orlov had brought with him. She was accompanied only
by one of her women, the faithful Shargorodskaya. Orlov
sat on the coach-box, beside Shkurin, the coachman, and off
they went at the gallop towards Petersburg. On the way
they encountered the Empress's hairdresser who used to
come to Peterhof every morning to dress Catherine's hair.
He, too, was taken along.

But Orlov had not thought of having fresh horses ready
on the sixteen-mile stretch separating Peterhof from the
Capital. In the end the exhausted animals slackened to almost walking pace, however hard they were driven. Fortunately, Gregory Orlov and Prince Bariatinsky who were
both worried for the Empress, had had the good idea of
coming to meet her, and encountered her five versts from
Petersburg. Catherine quickly entered their coach and soon
arrived at the barracks of the Ismailov Regiment.

Here, too, nobody was prepared for such stirring events,
and only a small number of soldiers was present. However,
that small band was roused and assembled; when they were
duly filled with vodka they were willing to cheer anyone.
Two of them were sent for a priest who arrived quickly and
also obliged: he raised the cross and mumbled the oath of
allegiance, the soldiers knelt and paid homage to the Empress as autocrat.

From here Catherine and her companions drove to the

barracks of the Preobrazhensky Regiment. Some initial resistance was encountered there, for Semyon Romanovitch Voronzov, a brother of Peter's mistress, was in command of one company and tried to defend the cause of the Czar and his sister. But soon Catherine's supporters gained the upper hand, and the entire regiment cheered her and swore the oath of allegiance. Grand Duke Paul was not mentioned. Voronzov and Major Voyekov broke their swords, indignant at this shameful betrayal of the oath sworn to the Czar. They were in danger of being lynched by the crowd. Voyekov saved himself by flight, while Voronzov was placed under close arrest. It was feared that he might ride to Oranienbaum and inform the Czar of what had happened in the Capital. Catherine later pardoned both officers, but never forgot. General Villebois of the Horse Guards, one of her most ardent supporters, reminded her of the great difficulties confronting so bold an undertaking. Catherine merely gave him a cold, proud look and said: "I have not sent for you to hear your advice. What are you going to do?" Then he, too, fell on his knees and paid homage to her.

Having gained the support of the troops, the Empress led them to the Church of Our Lady of Kazan, there to receive the oath of allegiance of her new subjects. Nikita Panin arrived, bringing with him eight-year old Paul who thus took part in his own deposition; for to him, not to his mother, was due the crown that was taken from Peter. It may have been Panin's intention to have Catherine proclaimed regent for her son; but he came too late.

The church was surrounded by 10,000 troops, many of them only partly dressed but all of them heavily armed. The Archbishop of Novgorod, the Razumovskys, Elizabeth's former favourites, Count Bruce, Count Stroganov, Prince Volkonsky and other dignitaries had arrived. Catherine was conducted in triumph to the Winter Palace, where the Senate and the Holy Synod were assembled. A crowd of courtiers bedecked with decorations thronged around the young Empress to kiss her hand. Only Chancellor Voronzov failed to understand what was happening, and naïvely asked the Empress why she had left Peterhof. Instead of replying she made a sign to lead him away. He was told to give the oath of allegiance in church, and he did so a few days later. His niece, Princess Catherine Romanovna Dashkov, was late in arriving at the Winter Palace. Her coach could not get through the vast throng of people that surrounded the Palace and filled the adjoining streets. When she finally reached the Palace, guardsmen carried her in triumph before the Empress, who embraced her affectionately and decorated her with the order of St. Catherine she herself was wearing.

In the meantime Teplov had drafted a manifesto for the Empress wherein Catherine laid particular stress on the dangers to the State and especially the Church, caused by Peter's government; and that he had been reckless in making peace with the "arch-enemy" (Frederick the Great). Various measures were then taken to make sure of all troops around the Capital. All roads were patrolled, and strong guards were placed on the road from Oranienbaum to Petersburg. A large part of the troops had so far believed the fictitious rumour of Peter's sudden death from a fall with his horse, but soon everybody learned that this was no regular succession but an act of force. Catherine's supporters were apprehensive lest there were fighting after all, for Peter had his Holstein troops with him in Oranienbaum. His person must be secured.

Meanwhile Peter had left Oranienbaum for Peterhof in order to discover for himself the truth of the many vague rumours that had reached him. He would not believe the news and, in utter confusion, searched every room in the palace for his wife. But the bird had flown. More reliable reports came and convinced him that Catherine had cast the die. His entourage, among them old Field-Marshal Münnich, advised him to go to Kronstadt, there to assure himself of the support of the garrison and the navy. But Peter at first rejected the suggestion. He was ready to defend Peterhof with his 1,500 Holstein troops and to meet his fate like a soldier. But in the end he gave in to Münnich's insistence and embarked for Kronstadt with his whole court, comprising a number of beautiful ladies, in a yacht and two boats. Trembling in all limbs he hid in the deepest hold of the vessel with Elizabeth Voronzov, his mistress.

The fortress-port was sighted at one in the morning. A sentry challenged the Imperial yacht. "The Czar".—"There is no Czar", came the answering call, "stand away!" Nevertheless Peter's advisers wanted him to land, being fully convinced that no one would dare to fire on the Czar. But Peter was a craven. Trembling with fright, he retraced his course. He had only one thought: to return safely to Oranienbaum with Elizabeth, there to await events.

When he got there, a fresh piece of unexpected news awaited him. Catherine, at the head of her troops, was marching against him and his Holsteiners.

For the Empress, it was a veritable triumphal march. She looked magnificent in the close-fitting uniform of the Syemyonov Guards she had borrowed from a young officer. She sat her horse well, and her long black hair flowed unrestrained over her shoulders. Her beautiful head, with its classic features, was adorned by a fur cap in which she wore a spray of oak leaves. Her beauty was dazzling. At her side rose young Princess Dashkov, still almost a child, wearing the same uniform and looking like a boy-subaltern. But both faces—that of the eighteen-year old girl and that of the more mature woman—shone with pride, ambition and daring. This was their victory, moral and political, over a man and an Emperor who was by far their inferior.

Peter III offered no resistance. The Empress's approach terrified him. He would not let her come to Oranienbaum but sent Prince Alexander Mikhailovitch Galitzin to meet her and to suggest that he should share the throne with her. Catherine did not even consider the proposal; her only reply was to send Peter an act of abdication for his signature. Meanwhile she continued her march. Not much later another emissary came from the Czar, General Ismailov, who informed her that Peter was willing to abdicate. Intimidated like a boy, Peter signed the document without resistance, thus sealing his doom.

In Peterhof, Catherine called a halt. She had the Czar and Elizabeth Voronzov brought before her. Peter behaved with an utter lack of dignity: he almost knelt before his wife, cried and sobbed and slobbered over her hand in abject humility. He begged not to be separated from his mistress. Catherine felt nothing but contempt for him and the Countess who knelt before her, crying as she saw the wreck of her ambitions.

In addition to his mistress, Peter asked for his dog, his negro, Narcissus, and his fiddle. He was granted these three wishes, but the Countess was removed to Moscow, where soon afterwards she married Prince Palliansky. The ex-Czar was ordered to reside at a country house at Ropcha, some sixteen miles from Petersburg. It was intended later to intern him in Russia's Bastille, the fortress of Schlüsselburg. His guard consisted of Prince Bariatinsky, Alexei Orlov and some other Guards officers, all of them among Catherine's foremost supporters. They were bold and unscrupulous, not afraid of any obstacle, any deed that might be necessary. In their hands now lay Peter's fate.

CHAPTER VII

The Assassination of Peter

CATHERINE HAD WON. On July 14/July 3 the new autocrat made her solemn entry into Petersburg. Now her position must be safeguarded. The least of her actions was being scrutinised, not only by Russia but by the whole world. But from the outset she knew how to overcome all difficulties, how to counter all dangers. The whole of Europe was full of praise for this daring Empress who emphasised the splendour of her reign with so much pomp and circumstance. She became the resplendent, open-handed ruler of an oriental country. A wealth of treasure ran through her fingers. During the first months of her reign she distributed immense amounts among those who had helped her to attain the throne and those whose friendship she wished to secure. Ever since her first hour in Russia, even as a child, she realised that there more than anywhere else gold can buy services, devotion and affection; that nowhere more than in Russia pleasantness and flattery have their effect. No one near Catherine could ever complain of a harsh word from her: to each she would address some pleasant remark, some joke or encouragement as she walked through rows of admiring courtiers. Even on the very first days of her reign, with official business and not a few worries almost overwhelming her, her mien was ever friendly and pleasant. Her personality fascinated everyone who came near her. People immediately noticed the great difference between her on the one hand, and Elizabeth's vacillating indolence or Peter's unreasonable, moody despotism on the other. Catherine's consummate adroitness in avoiding or mastering difficult situations and her genius for government evoked universal admiration.

The first few days of her reign left her with hardly a minute to herself. Cabinet and Senate meetings, audiences, public functions followed each other; manifestoes, ukases, decrees, new constitutions had to be issued, hundreds of petitions to be dealt with every day. But that great, ambitious woman showed no fatigue, no faltering, and mastered everything. In addition, her troops clamoured for her to appear on the balcony at all hours of day and night, for they feared lest a second coup d'état might take away their 'little mother'.

Catherine, however, held the reins of power in a firm grasp. It was a political event of another nature that might have aroused Petersburg, four days after the Empress's solemn entry, had the citizens known the true facts.

On July 18/7—Catherine had just left the Senate and in her room was changing her dress for an evening reception—Alexei Orlov rushed in and with great excitement reported that Peter was dead. Catherine turned pale. The smile left her face. She frowned, as she did when angry or annoyed. She sensed that no natural death could so conveniently have taken her husband. True, Alexei assured her with all earnestness that Peter had died of a "complicated haemorrhoidal colic" that had affected his brain; but neither Catherine nor Orlov himself or her wider entourage believed this fiction. This is proved by the fact that the Empress hurriedly summoned her Privy Council and decided to keep the event secret for another twenty-four hours.

On this occasion, too, she proved herself an accomplished actress. A short time after Alexei had brought her the shocking news she appeared amid her Court as usual, smiling amiably, joking easily, in full command of all her faculties and without a trace of emotion. It was only on the next day, a manifesto having announced Peter's sudden death, that Catherine wept bitterly in public and did not appear at Court. She acted the sorrowing widow, as convention and ceremonial required. Catherine always paid formal observance to etiquette. This did not, however, prevent her from denying her dead husband the full honours due to a Czar about to be interred. The body lay in state for three days, but without special pomp, dressed in the gala uniform of Holstein, its hands encased in white gloves on which witnesses claim to have seen traces of blood. The head was bandaged so as to be completely unrecognisable. Unlike other Russian Czars, the body was then not interred in the fortress but taken to the Monastery of Alexander Nevsky, where his tomb fell into oblivion. Her son, his mother's terrible hater, had his father's remains exhumed thirty-five years later on his mother's death as a frightful accusation against her. He had the dead Czar crowned and accorded him the same honours as to the recently deceased Empress. As a supreme gesture of irony he then had them buried side by side, as if nothing had ever come between them in their lifetimes.

Catherine was a great woman; but her glory was tarnished by the ever-present suspicion of complicity in her husband's murder. Even to-day, some doubt remains. She did nothing to allay such doubts, for none of the participants in the drama was prosecuted or punished. On the contrary: those present during Peter's last hours attained honours and dignities. Thus she accepted the accomplished fact, if not the intention.

This is not the place for historical research into Catherine's guilty knowledge of this regrettable happening, or into the actual cause of Peter's death. We are entitled to assume that the Orlovs were the real authors of the crime. Alexis Orlov, Teplov and the other officers guarding the royal prisoner are said to have made him drunk at supper and then to have poisoned him. Others, basing their opinion on a letter from Alexis to the Empress, written immediately after the deed, think that during a drinking bout when all, including Peter, were drunk, Alexis strangled the Czar with his own hands. What is certain is that the Orlovs had the greatest interest in removing Peter for good. This would free Catherine from the chains of matrimony and enable her to marry a man who might share her power. Gregory Orlov had sufficient imagination to see himself on the throne at Catherine's side. Active participation in Peter's murder, however, would have compromised him too much; it is for this reason that his brother Alexei may have assumed the principal rôle.

Even though Catherine may have contemplated closer ties with Orlov, she did not allow love to dominate affairs of state. Her sensuality was relegated to the place where it belonged—her bedroom; it did not enter the council chamber. Catherine was now the sole ruler; she did not require a consort. On the other hand she openly introduced a system of favouritism such as never before had been seen at a queen's court. The favourite became a special court official, an appointment endowed with a large salary, honours, dignities, titles and a luxuriously appointed apartment close to her own rooms. Of all offices under Catherine, this one received her greatest personal attention, while its holders displayed the most assiduous devotion to duty. With rare exceptions that post never remained vacant for more than twenty-four hours. Often a passing illness, a brief absence of the reigning favourite would suffice to have him replaced. Catherine took care that no men but those best qualified obtained that post. She might make mistakes in selecting her ministers, but when it came to appointing her 'personal aide-de-camp'—this was the favourite's official designation—she knew how to pick them.

More than twelve of these official favourites replaced one another during the reign of this remarkable woman. Men remained her favourite hobby well into her old age, yet she was neither hysterical nor a pervert. Some of her lovers, like Orlov, Potiomkin, Lanskoy, Zubov, had ambition, daring, understanding, and sometimes wit and sentiment. Their influence occasionally extended beyond Catherine's heart and into her politics. The rule of others was restricted to her bedroom. Some of them retained the Empress's friendship to the end, long after they had ceased to be her lovers, and continued to share all joys and sorrows of her heart. In this way she went on for a long time writing to Poniatovsky about all details of her amorous conquests, and later made her beloved Potiomkin the confidant of her amours. Towards those who for a time had shared her intimacy she usually remained grateful and well-affected even after their services had lost their purely personal character. They could be certain of attaining the highest dignities and were showered with wealth and favours.

These favourites on the retired list would usually spend some years abroad, unfolding their Asiatic wealth before the eyes of an astonished world and wasting their riches like true Orientals. Returning to Russia on their Mistress's behest they would either live quietly on the vast estates Catherine's liberality had provided for them, or they would occupy some high office at Court. They continued as her friends, honoured and respected by all—at least while Catherine lived. Never did she punish or hate one of her retired 'personal aide-de-camps', though it was not always she who dismissed them. There were some, like Mamonov, who wearied of her love or even rejected it outright. Even they did not have to fear Catherine's vengeance. Only one of her lovers did she humiliate, after having elevated him to the highest degree of splendour and power—a throne. Poniatovsky, the tender lover of her youth, whose knightly, passionate, admiring love formed Catherine's dearest memory—he alone was ignominiously humbled by his former love. She had seen him weak and timid as a king; and Catherine despised weaklings and cowards both in everyday life and in politics. Indulgent and forbearing in matters of love, she was inexorable and severe in matters political. She ordered her former lover to Petersburg, there to display in public his lost greatness.

Pride, vaingloriousness, ambition and conceit were her dominant passions; her sensuality took second place, despite the seeming contradiction of her life. She never allowed sentiment to master her. Her genius, her mind, her statesmanship dominated her innate passions and her intimate life.

Though indulging in voluptuousness more than any other woman, she ruled her vast dominions with admirable skill. Much in her life was pretence, but she rendered it convincing. She was impressive in everything she did; people did not know what to admire more, her qualities as a statesman or as a woman. There was universal enthusiasm over her boundless kindness, her irresistible charm and her personal beauty. Kings, statesmen, sages, philosophers and poets—they all recognised their equal in her. Voltaire did not know what to admire more, her great political acts or her literary works. Diderot falls into lyrical ecstasy as he writes admiringly: "Great Princess, I prostrate myself at your feet, I extend my arms, I want to speak: but my heart leaps, my head reels, my thoughts spin, I am discomfited

like a child. As by themselves, my fingers sound the ancient
lute, and I must sing:

> *Vous qui de la divinité*
> *nous montrez, sur le trône, une image fidèle . . ."*

Even Frederick the Great, who as a rule did not like
women on the throne, recognised the Great Catherine's
genius. All were enraptured either by her charms and pre-
possessing appearance or by her eminent talents, her vast
mental superiority, her will-power, the independence and
sureness of her judgment, and her untiring energy. Her
genius placed its stamp on her appearance. Though of short
stature, she seemed tall, impressive, majestic when presid-
ing over her court. Madame Vigée-Lebrun, the famous
paintress, was amazed by this phenomenon. When Count
Ségur had his first audience of Catherine, he began by
finding much about her theatrical and devised with an eye
on effect; but soon he too was fascinated by this remarkable woman. Only very rarely have Catherine's contemporaries recorded derogatory impressions of her. The only
thing for which she was reproached was an excessive, arrogant optimism. She was convinced that she must succeed
in everything, that all obstacles in her path were bound to
collapse.

She was not going to introduce into Russia reforms as
radical as those of Peter the Great. With her sound common-sense she realised from the outset that the changes
required in order to make something completely new out
of her immense realm would be too great, too radical. For
this reason her government was one of the cleverest ever
seen in Russia: she proceeded in complete conformity with
the ideas of her age and of her country. Though Catherine
did not possess the gift of picking eminent statesmen as
her advisers—Panin, her first Minister, was no more than

average—she had the invaluable knack of exploiting her servants and drawing the greatest advantage from their services. This she achieved merely through her pleasant approach, flattery, and the truly fabulous manner in which she rewarded services with riches and distinctions. This generosity may have contained an element of wastefulness at the expense of the state, but by this means she made herself devoted friends and supporters of her power and popularity. Her generals, some of whom were men of genius and enterprise, faced death for her with enthusiasm. She never reproached a man for a defeat or some ill-considered act of diplomacy: she would encourage him to fresh endeavours and assure him of imminent and glorious reinstatement. The culprits consequently felt doubly constrained to do everything in their power to make amends. Her indestructible optimism in the end infected her generals and her statesmen. If they suffered military defeat she would regard it as an 'insignificant contretemps', a mere nothing that did not count. The least success of her arms, on the other hand, became a glorious, splendid victory, and she never failed to proclaim it loudly to the whole world and to sing the praises of her incomparable generals and soldiers.

Catherine said of herself that she conducted her policies haphazardly and without a master plan. Yet even though her foreign policies were not always well-planned, she never lacked good sound sense. She sent her armies only against states trembling on the verge of downfall, thus remaining ever victorious. Her fame, her realm, her treasure attain undreamt-of height: the Semiramis of the North is at the summit of her power. She visits her vast domains like a Faery Queen, and everywhere her eyes see nothing but spendour, glory wealth and progress. All is not true; much is pretence. Potiomkin, the great 'manager', prepares his

Mistress's travels. The barge that carries Catherine down the Dnieper has on board the highest personalities, the leading men of science and economy, so that the Empress shall see for herself the wealth of wisdom Russia can produce. All along the river bank a magic spell has created new towns, villages and hamlets. A multitude of inhabitants throngs the bank, jubilantly to cheer the barge that carries Russia's 'little mother'. The fields are well kept; they are a joy to behold. Immense flocks graze in the pastures—yet all is pretence, a stage illusion. Potiomkin, the imaginative Taurian, has conjured it all up for a few days. From the populous districts of Little Russia, from places the Empress was not going to visit on her travels, he had forcibly brought the inhabitants to the desolate banks of the Dnieper. In this manner thousands of villages in Little Russia were for a time depopulated, the peasants and their flocks being dragged to the various regions traversed by Catherine. Sham villages and towns were put up, with attractive-looking wooden frames as houses. The Empress's journey over, the unfortunate people were driven back to their homesteads, many of them perishing in the process. But Catherine had the satismaction of seeing for herself how happy and prosperous were her country and her people.

Is was nevertheless good policy on Catherine's part to surround her reign and her throne with such extraordinary splendour. It served to hide the relative savagery of the country and most of its inhabitants. With great cleverness she managed to convey to the foreigner at her court the illusion of living in the most civilised of cities, the most cultured of courts, and an advanced and educated country. Without this, Russia would hardly have established full contact with Europe, and this, in turn, is the achievement for which Catherine rightly deserves the epithet of "Great".

CHAPTER VIII

The Favourites

1. *Gregory Orlov*

"RUSSIA IS SO USED TO FAVOURITISM", Count Solms wrote to Frederick the Great, "that no one there is surprised at the sudden elevation of some man; people even approve the choice of a gentle, polite youngster who shows neither ambition nor vanity." This "polite, gentle youngster" was Count Gregory Orlov! Frederick's Ambassador at the Court of Russia must have been a bad judge of character, for Gregory was anything but gentle. True, his innate indolence caused him to take little interest in the work Catherine gave him, but his ambition was sufficiently developed to let him wish and hope that his beloved would share her throne with him. This was the goal of his ambitions, and this was the sole reason for his part in placing Catherine on the throne of Russia. Once his chances in this respect had failed it was only on rare occasions that he felt obliged to display ambition. Yet he was not a man to be satisfied with the modest function of 'personal aide-de-camp', to be confined to the Empress's inner chambers. Catherine herself had no intention of letting her first 'official' lover wilt in the darkness of her bedchamber. The greater her passion for Gregory Orlov, the greater her endeavour to publicize her relations with him, to get him talked about. There was a great deal of vanity in the fact that she showed herself

more and more often in public in the company of this handsome man "whom nature had showered with her choicest
gifts". When she went for a drive he would sit by her side.
In the end he combined in his person all those honours and
powers that only Potiomkin and Zubov were to attain after
him. In addition to his official annual salary of 150,000
roubles, Catherine poured riches into his lap. Moreover, he
could draw on the exchequer at will; the millions that ran
through Orlov's hands have never been counted. He was
also one of the few who could openly wear the Empress's
likeness on his breast: he had her miniature set in a huge
diamond which he wore for years.

When Gregory Orlov assumed the function of official
favourite he received first of all the Chamberlain's key and
the Order of Alexander Nevsky. Then he and his four
brothers were made Counts. In quick succession he became
Catherine's chief aide de camp, Director-General of Fortifi-
cations, head of the Chevalier Guards, Lieutenant-Colonel
of the Horse Guards, Quartermaster-General, Knight of the
Blue Ribbon of Russia, and finally a Prince of the Realm.
He owned the finest palaces. Catherine gave him the Sten-
gelmann Palace on the Moika in Petersburg, the imperial
estates of Ropcha and Gatchina, various estates in Livonia
and Esthonia and other regions of Russia. Most splendid
of all was the celebrated marble palace over whose portal
she engraved the significant inscription: "In grateful
friendship".

Catherine did owe him some gratitude. It was partly
from his hand that she had received the crown; he had
staked his life to rescue her from the danger in which she
found herself after Elizabeth's death. She was passionately
devoted to him and loved him, not only for his beauty but
also for other qualities; his quick perception and his bold,
free-and-easy behaviour. A few months prior to the cata-

strophe, in April, 1762 and during the greatest crisis in her life, she bore Orlov a son. Originally named Alexei Romanov, he was later called Basil Gregorevitch Bobrinsky. Catherine had him brought up in the cadet corps and appointed Admiral Ribas his tutor. This child interested her far more than did the heir to the throne. She could often be seen driving to the cadet barracks, heavily veiled and in a plain coach without insignia and footmen, in order to ascertain her son's well-being. Yet the child was to be no joy to her. At the age of twenty, young Bobrinsky led a loose life abroad. He got into all sorts of scrapes and incurred ruinous debts which good old Grimm, the "long-suffering", had to settle at Catherine's orders. She put her spendthrift son in charge of a guardian and later interned him in Reval. Two daughters also resulted from Catherine's relations with Orlov, but were not officially recognised. They were brought up as her 'nieces' by Madame Protassov, Mistress of the Robes, later appointed ladies-in-waiting to their own mother, and married off.

The greater Catherine's renown and power, the more freely did she give rein to her feelings for Orlov who, in turn, was extremely indiscreet. He came to her at any hour of day or night, and in public treated the Empress with so much familiarity that even his intimates became somewhat apprehensive. When he had 'drink taken' he would openly boast of Catherine's favours and of the part he had played in helping her on the throne. He preened himself as the most powerful man in Russia who, if he wanted to, could destroy all of Catherine's splendour with one blow—an empty boast, this, for he would have ruined himself.

Catherine usually came to hear of these idle boastings, but only laughed, while Orlov rose in her favour from day to day. He abused his position to damage others, and his haughty arrogance towards everyone became insufferable.

ORLOV

Orlov lived in a dream, on a dizzy pinnacle amid the intoxicating atmosphere of a glittering court, the first man in
the country after the Empress, lover and beloved of a
beautiful woman, who was a ruler of genius. Catherine
could not be without him and suffered when they were
apart. Conscious of being irreplaceable he soon disregarded
Catherine's feelings and resumed his former life of a licentious Guards officer. He kept several mistresses in Petersburg without making a great secret of the fact. He would
spend weeks on end on bear-hunting trips, always accompanied by one or more women. Yet however blatant his
escapades, Catherine always remained indulgent. Only occasionally would she get her own back by indulging in some
infidelity of her own, as if to show him that his influence
was not quite so unshaken as he seemed to think. In these
little escapades she was abetted by Nikita Panin who would
have liked to have ousted his arrogant rival. It was due to
his efforts that Catherine, in Orlov's absence, received a
handsome young officer named Visotzky, on whom she had
had her eye for some time past. In this way Catherine
revenged herself for Orlov's neglect.

Her inflammable heart was about to blaze up in a fresh
passion when Orlov reappeared and exerted all his brutal
power to regain her favour. This was not difficult: he knew
how to be indispensable, and Catherine was passionately
in love with him despite everijthing. The new *vremyentchik* (man of the moment) was dismissed with a lavish
reward and a high position in some distant province.

Restored in his mistress's favour, Orlov did not bother
to mend his inconsiderate ways. Few women would have
been as forbearing as Catherine proved herself. In 1762,
Bérenger reported to the Duke de Praslin from Petersburg
concerning Orlov: "This Russian publicly violates the law
of the Empress's love. He has several mistresses in Peters-

burg. But far from incurring the Empress's wrath because of their complaisance towards Orlov, those ladies profit from it. When Senator Muraviev surprised his wife in Orlov's arms and threatened a public scandal by divorcing her, the Empress pacified him by presenting him with large estates in Livonia."

It is remarkable how pliable and submissive the great Catherine was in her love life, and how indulgent she was towards men who were by far her mental inferiors. In those hours she was a voluptuous woman—nothing else. Her political activities, her energy and enterprise in matters of state were not involved. It even amused her that the man she loved hardly understood her genius. Gregory Orlov, indolent by nature, never found one word of recognition for her achievements as a monarch, whereas she was always full of praise for his physical charms—and the mental qualities he lacked. When she sent him to Foksani to negotiate peace with the Turks after Rumiantsov had conquered them, she wrote to Madame Bjelke: "Count Orlov, who is beyond doubt the most beautiful man of his time, must appear like an angel of peace to those clods. His retinue is resplendent, but I wager that he overshadows all of them. He is a unique personality, this envoy of peace; nature has favoured him in everything, both as regards his face and his mind and heart." On another occasion, writing to Madame Geoffrin, she is transported with delight because her lover, for the first time, has lauded her. "When your letter arrived Count Orlov happened to be in my room. You write that I am very industrious, working at my code of laws and my embroidery at the same time. He, notoriously lazy though possessing much wit and, of course, many talents, exclaimed: 'Yes, that is true.' This is the first time I hear praise from his lips, and I owe it to you, Madame." Catherine, we notice, is all woman. A little word of praise from her lover means the greatest happiness to the woman whose praises are being sung by the whole world.

Orlov dit not love Catherine. At first it was ambition and passion and later vanity that chained him to her—and more than a little calculation; for the Empress showed her affection not merely by enthusing over his handsome physique and his "angel face", but in a more tangible way. Orlov was a limitless spendthrift who never had enough. He wasted millions. As Inspector-General of Artillery alone he received two million roubles a year for improvements in that arm, but he did nothing, while millions ran through his hands. Catherine never asked him for an accounting. It almost seems as if she stood in awe of the lover who had raised her to the throne, and was afraid to utter the slightest rebuke. After all, Orlov and his four brothers were a party and could not simply be pushed aside. This lack of assurance, combined with her unbounded passion for Gregory, often caused Catherine to appear weak where he was concerned. When he really rendered her some service, her gratitude and appreciation were overwhelming.

In time, though, she came to see the light. A woman of her mental eminence was bound to feel the shallowness of this man whose mind was filled with nothing but ostentatious fêtes designed to display his own physical strength and beauty; who, in his vanity and greed, basked in her reflected glory, amassed riches upon riches and behaved almost like a king. For ten long years the constant ardour of her love for him made her suffer everything, even his frequent infidelity. But the time came when she had enough. Her feelings lost their former intensity; her heart and her senses clamoured for a new lover, for fresh delights.

As soon as Orlov noticed his mistress's growing indifference he pulled himself together: once again he had to appear as her tower of strength, peerless and irreplaceable. In October, 1771, he had occasion to make sure of the Empress's eternal gratitude. For two months past a plague of smallpox had been ravaging Moscow, causing terrible mortality among the population. Although medical help had been sent the ignorant masses believed that the physicians and the authorities were spreading the pestilence. The furious populace rose, murdered the Bishop of Moscow and would have killed the Governor as well, had he not saved his life by flight. Some strong man must be sent there to restore order. Who was more suitable than the ruthless Orlov. He offered himself for this task, realising that no service he could render to Catherine could be greater or more likely to secure his position for ever. For the first time, however, the Empress let him go without a sign of regret, without a tear. Was she thinking of profiting by his absence in order to give him a successor? Gregory's star was visibly on the wane: the Empress's behaviour showed it. Her glance, roving among her courtiers, would sometimes rest longer than was strictly necessary on some fresh-faced young subaltern, some slender, courtly young diplomat.

But soon miraculous reports arrived from Moscow of Gregory's strong and effective measures. His wild ruthlessness succeeded in restoring order in the city, cowing the panicking populace into submission, and overcoming the pestilence by introducing sanitary measures. The plague had already carried off a hundred thousand Muscovites when Orlov appeared like a saviour. He made use of the expert knowledge of hygiene and medicine supplied by Todte, a German surgeon of great experience, and Counsellor Volkov, but the credit remained his. Orlov returned in triumph to Petersburg, where his mistress once again became his grateful admirer. She built a triumphal arch in Czarskoye Selo with the inscription, "To him who saved Moscow from the plague." She also had a medal struck on which Orlov's portrait was united with that of Curtius, inscribed, "Russia also has such sons."

Once again Gregory Orlov was her peerless paragon, "like one of the ancient Romans"; he was "unique, incomparable". No words could praise him sufficiently, no fête was sumptuous enough to honour him, no present too precious to reward him. Yet it was no longer the same ardour, the same passion that Catherine was feeling for this darling of fortune. A few months later he was once again sent on a mission, this time to Foksani, where he was to negotiate peace with the Turks. Conscious of his unequalled power, however, Orlov acted contrary to the wishes of the Empress and her Prime Minister. Far from beginning negotiations, he wanted to resume the war and to lead the army now standing on Turkish soil; his vanity would not suffer Rumiantsov, the real victor, to overshadow him. At a public session of the conference, in the presence of all diplomats, he violently quarrelled with Rumiantsov and finally shouted with his customary brutality that he would hang the old general. Thereupon he completely neglected public business; instead, he held his resplendent court at Jassy where lavish festivities were given every day. He appeared in a suit literally covered with diamonds: it had cost one million roubles. His generous mistress had paid him that amount in consideration of his efforts to negotiate an advantageous treaty. Perhaps she also wished thereby to prolong his absence while making him think that her heart was still all his. For in the meantime a fresh applicant for the post of personal aide-de-camp had made his appearance. Panin was still at work, doing his best to dislodge the hated favourite.

In the midst of his whirl of pleasure at Jassy Orlov learn-

ed that Catherine had given him a successor a fortnight
after his departure from Petersburg, and that she was so
much taken up with her new lover that she neglected affairs of state—something that had never happened before,
however great her new passion. But this time it had happened. She spent hours on end in her room with her new
favourite, an amiable young nonentity named Vassilchikov,
and seemed to have forgotten everything else. Orlov realised
that speedy action was required. Only his presence in Petersburg could prevent his ruin. He must stake everything
on one throw. He dropped everything, fêtes and peace negotiations, and threw himself into a *kibitka,* a light, open
carriage. In it, he raced across the steppes, travelling day
and night and hardly stopping for rest and refreshment.

A great disappointment awaited him. Only a few versts
from Petersburg he was stopped by an order from the
Empress, commanding him and his train to undergo four
weeks' quarantine, as they were coming from the South,
where the plague was still raging. He had not expected this.
It showed him Catherine's shrewd caution, and at the same
time made him feel her power: one order from her, and
he was made to realise that *she* was the Empress, and *he*
but her subject. Yet consideration and sweet reasonableness
coated the bitter pill. This quarantine was indispensable,
said Catherine, but she suggested he might spend it in his
own palace at Gatchina, that lovely spot which he himself
had described in a letter to Rousseau as "peaceful and made
for rêverie." Here Gregory Orlov could now dream of the
the past, of fallen greatness, lost splendour and departed
love. He had to obey. Young Vassiltchikov now enjoyed all
the advantages and favours that had been his. He had
found the means of ousting the handsome favourite and
attracting Catherine, at least for a time. It was a hard
blow for the vain, conceited man to be dismissed in this

abrupt manner. But he did not despair; his immense arrogance was still alive. Again we see in Catherine's behaviour that secret fear of the ruthless man whom she thought capable of anything. Might he not one night appear in the palace, in the rooms of her new favourite, and regain his former position by some desperate act of violence? Catherine must have had this in mind, for she doubled the sentries around the palace and had the locks of the doors changed. The road from Gatchina to Petersburg was closely guarded. Catherine lived in a state of permanent anxiety, yet she could not bring herself to say the one word that would have banished her importunate ex-lover for ever. It was with infinite tact and consideration that she suggested he might wish to resign from his other offices. But Orlov refused to resign; in vain did she, almost timidly, try to convince him that he must. Orlov refused to listen. In the end the Empress appeared almost apologetic for her faithlessness, and that to a man who had flagrantly and cynically deceived her hundreds of times.

Catharine was afraid of a last meeting with him. He begged, he entreated, he almost threatened—but in vain. She did not feel proof against this dangerous tempter who had dominated the woman in her. She anxiously avoided even the most casual meeting with him. During a masked ball at Court a sudden rumour spread that Count Orlov's coach had been seen entering the palace yard; the Empress, who had been promenading in gay mood arm in arm with Vassiltchikov, immediately took refuge in Panin's apartments. It was a false rumour, however, and she returned after some time; but she had received such a shock that the rest of the evening was spoilt.

It is understandable that she could not at one stroke dismiss from her life the man who had been living in closest intimacy with her for ten long years. Love was replaced by almost motherly care and friendship. She wrote to him often and at length. Like a mother she took care of his well-being, even of the smallest details of his daily life at Gatchina, where she would send him fresh linen. No bourgeois housewife could have been more solicitous than the great Empress. Other queens, less powerful than Catherine, got rid of their discarded lovers by banishment, or by the sword; Catherine negotiated with them and gave them advice how best to suffer separation and order their future lives. She consoled Orlov by telling him that this was but a temporary separation, for one year perhaps; during this period he was to live in Moscow, on his estates or wherever he wished.

She lacks the courage to dismiss the man to whom she owes so much. His salary as "personal aide-de-camp" goes on—150,000 roubles!—so that he may furnish a house in Moscow. Until this is ready, he has permission to live in any of her châteaux near Moscow, use court carriages and attendants, etc. She makes him a present of 4,000 souls as a reward for his victory at Tchesmé—a battle in which he did not take part, and adds another 6,000 serfs to that number. Her gifts to Orlov are truly princely: several silver services for daily use, valuable furniture, all the art treasures from his former lodgings in her palace, and a house in Troitskaya Pristanye—as though he were short of houses and palaces to live in. All this she did for her discarded lover; but he must not come to Petersburg.

There she was living in the first intoxication of a new passion. Vassiltchikov was young, good-looking and devoted to her. Always at Catherine's side, he sat with her at the gaming table, accompanied her on her drives and had unrestricted access to her private apartments. Yet he had not the slightest influence in matters of state. The Empress did not seem interested in giving him the education she had tried to impart to Orlov. In her early years with Orlov she had often read to him from good books, giving him much information on matters of politics, philosophy, literature and art, thus filling some of the gaps in his sketchy education. Vassiltchikov was different. He was not better read than Orlov and perhaps even less acute and perceptive, but Catherine seemed tired of supervising the intellectual education of her lovers. Vassiltchikov did not manage to gain much influence, even though the Empress treated him with great familiarity in public and conferred distinctions on him. Yet he did not lack influential advisers: Prince Bariatinsky and Nikita Panin did not fail to initiate him into all court intrigues; but Vassiltchikov did not manage to exploit his position. The only profit he derived from his position as favourite was Catherine's princely generosity in rewarding him for his loyal services.

This kind of rival was not dangerous to Orlov. By dint of persistence and audacity he finally managed to reappear at the Court of Petersburg. One day he just happened to be there, no one knew how, and whether the Empress had given her permission. He came invested with fresh glory, for on October 4, 1772 the Empress had made him a Prince, a title that was to recompense him for having lost the post of lover. Catherine's love had turned into friendship, and Orlov did not ask for more. His vanity was satisfied by being able to play some part at Court. Soon he was as influential as ever, except that he no longer possessed her heart. Again she lavished gifts upon him and flattered his adherents and friends, for his power was still dangerous.

Orlov, however, accepted his new role with better grace than might have been expected. The man who had been so arrogant, haughty and conceited towards everyone while he was in power now became the assiduous flatterer of the new favourite. He was constantly seen at Vassiltchikov's side, not caring how ridiculous he must appear. He seemed intent on being talked about, and his wastefulness knew no limits. He was more ruthless, more luxurious, more boastful than ever. He went so far as to show himself, completely drunk, near the palace in the company of prostitutes. The whole town talked of his scandals and the insolence with which he compromised the Empress. Yet she paid him marked attention, invited him to her card evenings and intimate parties, and on all occasions distinguished him. Her weakness for this man arose from her character: she wanted to convince the world that her gratitude exceeded even her passion. She herself remarked, while settling with the greatest care all details of Gregory Orlov's material welfare, that she was never going to forget the services rendered her by the Orlov family.

In 1773 Orlov spent some time at Reval. He gave brilliant fêtes, and behaved like the Empress's favourite; as before, he distributed decorations, promised official positions and dignities, and basked in the sunshine of his own glory. The following spring he returned to Petersburg and once more occupied all the positions he had held before, with the sole exception of that of favourite. No longer were Catherine's heart and senses engaged; love had no part in this rapprochement with her former lover. Policy alone induced her not to allow a man like Orlov to remain idle but to retain him in her service. Their relations were merely friendly, for Vassiltchikov still held the fort. Yet there were still ties between Orlov and Catherine that never broke. In 1776 she wrote to Grimm: "I have always felt inclined to accept guidance from people who knew more than I; but they must not allow me to discover that they are deliberately doing so, or I take instant flight. Of all the men I know, only Prince Orlov is apt to succour this weakness of mine. His is a mind that instinctively goes its own way, and mine follows him."

In later years she spoke of her other lovers with almost offensive indifference, but not of Orlov. To her, he ever remained the noblest, best and cleverest of men. At the age of forty-three he fell in love with his cousin, an attractive young maid-of-honour of Catherine's, Demoiselle Zinoviev, who was then nineteen years old. It was no superficial attachment but a deep and genuine feeling that for the first time in his life took hold of him; and Catherine had to admit that she had never had such pure love and devotion from him. Orlov changed completely. Dominated by this great and authentic emotion he lived only for his charming bride whom he married in disregard of the Greek Church's laws of consanguinity. The Senate ordered their separation; but now the Empress who had once loved that man showed herself truly great and noble. An intriguing or vindictive woman in her place would have begrudged him his happiness. Not so Catherine. She rescinded the Senate's decree, and Orlov, blissfully happy, could take his young bride to Switzerland. Romance had a tragic ending. Five years later, in 1782, the young Princess died of tuberculosis in Lausanne, Europe's most eminent physicians having proved powerless to cure her.

Orlov returned to Petersburg a changed man. He could not get over his wife's death. His sorrow and the effects of his former debauches induced a derangement of the brain under which he had been labouring for two years past. Orlov, dazzling Orlov, became insane. In his deranged mind the past revived. There were moments of terror when his darkened mind would see the phantom of the dead Czar. Then he screamed with horror, crawled into a corner and befouled his face with his own excrement in order to escape recognition by the accusing shadow. At long last, on

April 13, 1783, in Moscow, death released him from his misery. Rumour asserts that Potiomkin, Orlov's real successor in Catherine's favour, was believed to have poisoned him, using a herb called *pyanaya trava* which is said to derange the minds of those who eat it.

Catherine was shocked. Deep emotion overcame her as she learned of Orlov's death. Some tenderness for her erstwhile lover still remained, though ten years had passed since then and several others had succeeded him. A violent fever forced her to take to her bed, and she became so delirious during the night that she had to be bled. To Grimm she wrote: "Though I was fully prepared for this painful event I confess that I am deeply shaken. Consolation from others and what I tell myself is of no avail— sobs and tears are my reply, and I suffer terribly." Many years later, in her large correspondence with a variety of people, she always reverted to her old lover who in the end appeared a veritable genius in her memories. She praised his eminent talents, his resolution, his eloquence, his frankness and courtesy, drawing comparisons between him and Count Nikita Panin who died about the same time as Orlov. The comparison was always favourable to her lover.

Yet despite her admiration, tenderness and love for this man, this curious woman let his brother Alexis have intercourse with her, though for him she did not feel the same passion as for Gregory. Catherine bore Alexis a son, too; he received the name of Tchesmensky—son of the victor of Tchesmé. Posterity knows little of this son, for Catherine cared little for him. Devoted to sensual enjoyment, this woman had but the rudiments of the maternal instinct.

2.   *Potiomkin*

Not all of Catherine's favourites enjoyed the same free-

dom and power as Orlov. Not one of them could take the
liberties he did. Life in the palace was guided by strict
rules. Catherine had established regulations in conformity
with a system that protected her from a favourite's undue
preponderance and assured her of his loyalty. After Orlov,
only Potiomkin, Lanskoy and Zubov managed to shake off
these fetters of love. Few among Catherine's lovers dared
to nurse ambitions beyond their duties. So great were the
riches lavished on them and the honours and dignities per-
taining to the post of official favourite that the chosen
incumbent of that much envied position gladly gave up his
personal liberty. Catherine in consequence never lacked ap-
plicants for the job. It usually was filled in the following,
rather cold-blooded, way.

At night, after supper, when the Empress gathered her
court around her, Her Majesty would be seen taking a
marked interest in some handsome young Guards lieutenant. He must have well-turned legs and be well-built. She
liked tall, strong men, and only rarely picked a slight, delicate youth. If some young officer pleased her, information
was gathered concerning his disposition, mode of life and
character, and then he was commanded on some pretext to
wait upon the Empress. Most of them knew what this meant,
or had good friends to tell them of the good luck awaiting
them. Her Majesty's physician-in-ordinary would be present at the first audience and, after the newcomer was
presented to the Empress, would take him into an adjoining
room, there to subject him to a medical examination. This
test passed, the new favourite was installed in his official
residence, underneath the Empress's private apartments.
Both suites were connected by a secret staircase. The favourite's rooms were marked by lavish luxury and comfort;
they might have been intended for the spoilt mistress of
a King of France. A horde of servants waited upon the new

incumbent. He now bore the style and title of "personal aide-de-camp to the Empress", and the highest court dignitaries bowed to him. Yet the bearer of this impressive title was often a mere stripling in his early twenties who but the day before might have spent hours waiting in the antechambers of old generals and diplomats. But times change; yesterday poor and insignificant, he was to-day wealthy and powerful. In the bureau of his drawing-room lay 100,000 roubles in gold as a first present from his imperial mistress; for he must now equip himself as befits a prince. Only rarely did Catherine pick her lovers from among the wealthy aristocracy.

On the first night of his new status the favourite would appear at court arm in arm with Her Majesty, wearing the brand-new uniform of Adjutant-General. All eyes were turned on the lucky man, who may not have been completely at ease during these first few hours while his official duties were thus openly made clear. Fortunately this parade did not last long, for on such nights the Empress would retire to her bedroom before ten o'clock, followed by the new *vremyentchik*.

From now on he led the life of a prince. Every month he found twelve to fifteen thousand roubles "pin money" on his dressing table The Court Marshal was instructed daily to lay table for twenty-four people of his suite and to take care of all his household expenses. The favourite himself would dine at the Empress's table, mostly alone with her, or only with a small circle. Enjoying the greatest honours he was, next to Her Majesty, the most respected and feared person at court. But he was a captive bird— his plumage brilliant, his cage of gold, yet carefully guarded. Catherine's experience with faithless Orlov had been too upsetting. Her minor favourites therefore left the palace only with the Empress or accompanied by some

trustworthy persons selected by herself. They had to suffer the closest supervision and could not receive visitors
without Catherine's presence or knowledge. Neither could
they accept invitations without her permission. Jealously
she watched over each move, each act of the "man of the
moment". On one occasion Mamonov took a liberty. He
presented Catherine on her birthday with a pair of valuable
ear-rings that were greatly admired by Grand Duke Paul's
wife. Catherine immediately gave them to her. That night
the young Grand Duchess wore the ear-rings which, by
the way, had cost 30,000 roubles. Since she knew that
Mamonov had given them to the Empress she sent for him
next morning with the intention of thanking him as the
indirect donor. Mamonov was about to obey the Grand
Duchess's summons when Catherine learned of it and made
a terrible scene. The visit was cancelled. A few days later
Grand Duke Paul repaid the kindness by sending the favourite a diamond-studded snuff box. Now Catherine permitted her lover to thank her son for this attention, but
she sent someone in her confidence with him. The Grand
Duke refused to receive them.

Under such restraint Vassiltchikov, Orlov's successor,
spent two years, from 1772 to 1774. He was one of the
few not to abuse Catherine's favour. He did not enrich
himself from public funds, did no harm to anyone, kept
aloof from court intrigues and thus had neither enemies
nor detractors. Catherine praised his unassuming manner
and highly esteemed him for this quality so rare in courtiers. But suddenly she had enough of him. He bored her,
not only because he was commonplace but because he was
always even-tempered and knew no will but that of his
mistress. "I was no better than a kept woman", says Vassiltchikov of himself,—"and was treated as such. I could
neither have visitors nor go out. If I asked for something

on behalf of others I received no reply; if for myself, the result was the same. When I wanted the order of St. Anne I spoke to the Empress. The next day I found bank notes to the value of 30,000 roubles in my pocket. In this manner my mouth would be stopped, and I sent to my room."

One day that weak-willed man was ordered to go to Moscow, why, he did not know. He obeyed without demur, without demanding an explanation. Generous presents such as Catherine used to give to her discarded lovers consoled him for his fall from grace.

His place was taken by a man of greater strength and energy, a masterful and domineering character whose drive and genius were bound to impress a woman like Catherine—Potiomkin. At thirty-four, he was in the flower of virility and at the height of his powers.

Potiomkin had first crossed her path on that memorable day, unforgettable to Catherine: the 26th of June, 1762, when she was riding towards her destiny at the head and in the uniform of the Semyenovsky Regiment. The officer who had lent her his uniform had forgotten to give her his silver sword-knot. A young ensign of noble birth was standing nearby; he quickly undid his sword-belt and handed it to the Empress. He was Gregory Alexandrovitch Potiomkin, then twenty-two years old, the son of a poor Russian nobleman of Smolensk. He had received a scholarship and spent a few terms at Moscow university but had been sent down for "lack of application and frequent failure to attend lectures." His father having some contacts at Elizabeth's court, he chose an officer's career and managed to be admitted to the Semyonovsky Regiment. Chance put him in the path of the Orlovs and of the momentous events of the summer of 1762. Catherine did not forget the obliging young ensign, though his appearance had not struck her as particularly impressive; on August 1 she promoted him lieutenant. One month later he was received at her court and made a gentleman of the bedchamber—within the purely ceremonial meaning of that term. This quick promotion he owed to the Orlovs. They told the Empress of his great social talents, particularly of his gaiety, and of his amusing gift for mimicking anybody's voice to perfection. Catherine loved nothing better than jolly company, and people who amused her were always welcome. Thus young Potiomkin joined the circle of her intimates. The Empress was highly amused and entertained by his incomparable mimicry and brilliant wit. She laughed till the tears came to her eyes when he imitated her own diction and voice. Potiomkin was not afraid to give a close impersonation of his august monarch. Catherine in her circle of friends was much too human and companionable to have resented mockery. Yet it seemed as though in his case her foresight saw further than in regard to other men singled out by her. She seemed to sense Potiomkin's rich talents and genius, though they were still dormant; she must have had a presentiment that this young man was one day going to play whatever part she would exact from him. From this moment she took care of his further education and development. In a ukase of 1763 she recommended the Senate to initiate her "young pupil" Gregory Alexandrovitch Potiomkin into all branches of statecraft and to this end to place him in one of the Senate offices. As his tutor and adviser she appointed the Count du Vivarais who was later to serve as secretary to the great and influential favourite.

At that time, however, Gregory Potiomkin made no further personal progress in his amiable patroness's favours. For some years to come Orlov was to remain sole ruler. Potiomkin, young and headstrong, was unwise enough to incur the enmity of the two Orlovs. One day, over a game of billiards, he had a violent quarrel with Alexis; a fight ensued, and in the brawl giant Orlov knocked out one of Potiomkin's eyes.

Thus disfigured, Potiomkin felt no longer able to appear at court. He took part in the Turkish wars, not to his disadvantage. He rose at great speed and became a Lieutenant-General when only thirty-three. Catherine had not forgotten her protégé.

Ten years had passed since her first meeting with Potiomkin. The desire to obtain his Empress's highest favours grew ever stronger in the young officer's heart, and with it the wish to oust handsome Orlov. This, however, seemed unlikely. Another man became Catherine's favourite, while her sole intention concerning Potiomkin seemed to be to make him a useful collaborator.

But Potiomkin did not give up. He knew Catherine's greatest feminine failing, her vanity. He knew that no flattery was more effective than to pretend to be head over ears in love with her: one who had dared to raise his eyes too high was going to retire, love's cruel wounds deep in his heart, to fall on a stricken field or—to earn her favour. Potiomkin the fanciful went even further in his deliberate sentimentality. He talked of giving up the world and living as a monk, to pay homage in pious seclusion to the august beloved of his hapless heart.

Catherine was credulous in matters of love. All her life she allowed herself to be gulled by men who talked to her of love. She fully believed that Gregory Potiomkin was going to "get him to a 'monkery'," as he had told his friends. Besides, it was something new that a man was going to renounce the world for love of her. That woman of forty-four was attracted by the sentimental aspect of Potiomkin's love. Ever since Zachar Chernichev and Poniatovsky she had missed a tender attachment. And then—was not Potiomkin's genius equal to her own? The name of the victor of Silistria was soon on everybody's lips. He was spoken of as a hero and general of genius. What was Vassiltchikov against him? A nonentity, a pliable tool. Catherine longed for a meeting with a man who with physical strength and passion would combine genius, intelligence, character and a certain warmth of feeling. She was now tired of insignificant Vassiltchikov and giving way to a spontaneous desire wrote to Potiomkin towards the end of 1773:

"It appears that you are so much preoccupied with Silistria that you seem to have no time to read letters. I do not know as yet if your bombardment has been successful. Nevertheless I am convinced that everything you undertake arises from your zeal for my person and for our beloved country which you serve so well. But since I am anxious to preserve zealous, brave, intelligent and able men I beg you not to expose yourself to unnecessary risks. In reading this letter you may ask why it was written. I can only say: in order to prove to you how much I think of you, for I always wish you all that is good."

Clearer language was not needed. Potiomkin understood that his time had arrived. He left the South and arrived at Catherine's court in Petersburg in January, 1774. But six weeks were to pass before he could establish his position. Potiomkin did not want to risk defeat. He reconnoitred the terrain and found it suitable for his proposed operation. On February 27 he took the decisive step, aiming straight for his goal and without employing circumlocution. He simply wrote to the Empress, asking her if she thought him worthy to be appointed her "personal adjutant". The reply was favourable. The next day he occupied the favourite's apartments like a veritable conqueror, thus holding at last the field that he had been denied so long.

Catherine was delighted with her new acquisition. Potiomkin's features were unprepossessing and disfigured—the Orlovs called him "Cyclops"—but in his love there was something she had not known before: sentimentality. Neither Orlov nor Vassiltchikov had it. Potiomkin, though no longer a youth, would kneel before her in transports of ecstasy, admiring her beauty, whispering tender nothings into her ear, full of a happiness that was both genuine and convincing. His boundless passion, his giant stature, his boldness in new forms of dalliance enchanted the Empress. He was the first man in years to have dared being first to speak of his love—a man's privilege that even an Empress could not deny him. Catherine was proud and happy to be loved; for in his romantic way Potiomkin was really in love with her. Hitherto it had always been she who had lavished attentions and presents on her lovers; but this man, even though his beloved was an empress, was not a mere recipient of gifts. To him, nothing was too good, too rare or precious to put at Catherine's feet. One of his officers named Bauer was for ever travelling, scouring the world for rare curios with which Potiomkin surprised the Empress. He would send Bauer, now to Paris, now to Astrakhan, Poland, the Crimea, either to fetch a dancer, a special kind of water melon, rare grapes or even flowers. As another man in love would send his servant about the town to get some precious trifle for his beloved, so did this fantastic lover send his faithful servant on a tour of the world.

In Catherine he adored both the beloved woman and his' Empress. He loved her as he loved his fame. She in turn entertained the greatest admiration for his remarkable talents and his singular versatility. When Grimm gently reproached her for frequently changing her favourites she replied: "Why do you reproach me; because I dismiss a well-meaning but very boring little man (Vassiltchikov) in

POTIOMKIN

favour of one of the most comical and amusing originals of this iron century?" And when Potiomkin in 1774 concluded the peace treaty of Kütchük-Kainardje with the Turks, she wrote to her "souffre-douleur:" *"Ah! que c'est une bonne tête que cet homme-là! Il a plus de part que personne à cette paix, et cette bonne tête est amusante comme le diable."* (What a good head that man has on his shoulders; no one deserves greater credit for this peace than he, and this clever fellow is as amusing as the devil). On another occasion she is convinced that he is much cleverer than she, and that everything he does is part of a well-laid plan. In fact, Catherine's mental energy far surpassed her lover's.

Yet they were an excellent match, these two, both of them people of rare genius. Potiomkin was a veritable demon in his polarity, creating, destroying and filling everything with fresh life. His spendthrift luxury far surpassed that of the Orlovs. Immense sums were at his disposal. He commanded all state funds, delving freely into them, but used the money largely for the benefit of the empire. His personality was so tremendous in its powerful impact that even in his absence he completely dominated the scene. A queer mixture of genius and cynical brutality, European education and refinement on the one hand and Asiatic barbarism on the other; of selfishness and humanity, energy and sluggishness, industry and laziness, he was the typical Russian intellectual. The Prince of Ligne once said that his all-embracing genius would be enough for a hundred ordinary people. Even his enemies deferred to him. He understood the art of making friends to perfection so that later, when ambition and friendship had replaced their passionate attachment, his influence at Catherine's court remained unchanged and all continued to bow to him, even the Empress's lovers of the hour.

"She is madly in love with Potiomkin", said Senator Yellagin to Durand, "and they are bound to love each other, for they are completely similar." Catherine's letters to her lover indeed display a tenderness far exceeding the usual style in which queens write to their favourites. Towards no other lover did she use the tender words addressed to Potiomkin, pet names like *galubtchik* (little dove), dear soul, love bird, my beloved, dearest heart, etc. As among ordinary people, lovers' quarrels and slight bouts of jealousy occurred between the loving Empress and her lover. Potiomkin was not easy to live with; he was defiant and sulky or flew into a temper and smashed things. For days on end he would sulk in silence; then Catherine, her eyes red with tears, sat silently at table with him. Or she would write to him: "If you are not more amiable to-day than yesterday, I ... I ..., forsooth, I shall not eat." But they always made it up again, however serious their quarrel, for they both firmly believed in the all-enduring quality of their love. After one such quarrel he wrote to her: "Allow me, dear soul, lastly to tell you how I think our quarrel is going to end. Do not think that I am worrying about our love. In addition to the countless benefactions which you have lavished on me you have granted me a place in your heart. I want to be alone in it, above all those who have come before me, since none of them has loved you as I love you. And since I am the work of your hands, I want to see you have a rest. I want you to enjoy the benefactions you are heaping upon me, and to find some relief from the heavy labours imposed on you by your exalted position."

A different and deeper language, this, than Orlov's whom Catherine had to drive to any active work. Potiomkin, however, realised that her passion was fleeting; that to-morrow he might be ousted from her private rooms. It was his energy, his statesmanship, his generalship, his gifts as administrator and organiser, in brief, his position as her friend, adviser and pillar of strength that must assure his prominence. At the same time he knew how to speak to Catherine's heart, to be the ardent, tender lover who adored the woman and the sovereign. He never forget the respect he owed to the Empress. For her he gave the most sumptuous entertainments ever seen at the court of Russia, for his private wealth was immense. In his palaces at Krementchug and Kherson he lived like a satrap. The Taurian Palace was the scene of dazzling lavishness and splendour. Potiomkin liked the joys of the table as well as wine; in Petersburg, Kiev and Jassy his table bore the choicest meats. Yet he was no true gourmet; he liked plenty of good food and drink when it could be had, but when necessary was satisfied with some bread and a bit of garlic. He would drink dozens of bottles of *kvass* every day and, rising from the Empress's table, eat a raw turnip with great relish.

His clothes were as bizarre as his habits. His usual dress was a voluminous dressing-gown which he did not exchange for more suitable raiment even when receiving lady visitors. He would wear it even when giving dinners and receptions on his travels through his provinces. Underneath this commodious garment he wore neither shirt nor breeches. His visitors would find him thus semi-nude stretched on his couch, apparently sunk in idle rêverie. Yet his numerous manuscript letters to officials whose labours he supervised, the many memorials and other papers from his hand are the best proof of his organising ability and uncommon application.

He would often appear in Catherine's apartments dirty, barefoot, scantily dressed. His long hair was unkempt, his nails neither clean nor cut short but bitten, an unpleasant habit in which he indulged freely before the Empress and the court. One of the rules of the "Ermitage", Catherine's circle of intimates where almost anything "went", seemed aimed at Potiomkin; it read: "Visitors are requested to make merry without destroying, smashing or biting things."

It was only on very important occasions that Potiomkin could be induced to shed his robe. He would then fall into the other extreme and make his appearance in fantastic uniforms, studded with gold and diamonds, which he designed himself. Huge plumes crowned his head, and his breast was covered with medals and decorations.

Catherine knew all the weaknesses and faults of the man, but she truly admired him. She may have loved others more tenderly than Potiomkin, but for no other man did she ever feel such friendship and admiration. None of them had asserted himself to such an extent; yet Catherine still remained his superior. Like Orlov, Potiomkin coveted the throne, and with greater justification. He hoped that Catherine would place the seal of the church upon their union; but he was mistaken. Her love did not go so far as to make her give up her independence.

Catherine's physical relations with Potiomkin lasted only two years. In 1776, while her lover was on a trip to Novgorod, she placed young Peter Zavadovsky in the golden cage near her apartments. He had been her secretary, and his well-knit figure attracted her interest. Zavadovsky, however, was aiming higher. He planned nothing less than to displace completely the powerful Prime Minister, Potiomkin.

Neither he nor Catherine, who was otherwise so adept at getting rid of "faded pictures", had counted with Potiomkin's hard head. He was no Orlov, to make a virtue of necessity and to recover by devious ways the honours and dignities taken from him by his mistress's whim. Potiomkin came back and asserted his mastery. He was not the man to be cast aside like a discarded garment. An emotional scene took place between him and the Empress. He roared like a lion and smashed everything in sight. As frequently on such occasions, Catherine got the worst of it and submitted to his will.

Yet Potiomkin did not seek to recover his former place in the inner chambers that another had usurped in his absence. He could not be the successor of a Zavadovsky. But he wanted to remain her adviser, minister and general, and suffered no one to deprive him of his power and his influence in affairs of state. His ambition and vanity would never have permitted it. His eyes rose even higher: he dreamed of the crown of Courland as a sop for love rejected. Catherine, however, was no longer in a position to give away crowns. Yet she understood that this darling of fortune, the man she herself had coddled and idolised, could not bear the slightest diminution of his position or her confidence. She could not deprive of his power in the state this extraordinary character who was "part giant, part romantic hero, part barbarian." She needed him. And so Potiomkin remained the pseudo-Czar, as the people called him.

Outwardly as well as privately he retained his power. No new favourite from now on entered the inner sanctum without Potiomkin's consent. He was his sovereign's *"maître de plaisir"*. If he was no longer the favourite he at least took care that the men who were to provide Catherine with the distractions he was no longer allowed to furnish should be completely subordinate to him. Zavadovsky was not fortunate enough to please the mighty man. Catherine, too, may not have been over-fond of him, for the demands of her voluptuousness had risen to excess with the years. Zavadovsky would at times forget his proper task and cherished ambitious plans—in brief, he fell from favour and was dismissed. However, his eighteen months' reign as favourite had procured him some remarkable advantages, and curiously enough, he continued to hold high office even after his dismissal from the Empress's personal service. Catherine lavished riches and distinctions upon him, and even long after her death he was to feel the happy benefits of past favour. In 1794 Emperor Francis II of Austria made him and his two brothers Princes of the Realm, and three years later Catherine's son, Czar Paul, promoted him Count. Under Alexander I Zavadovsky became Minister of Public Instruction.

Potiomkin took care to change the incumbent of the favourite's office at frequent intervals, thus probably meeting his sovereign's tastes and desires. Zavadovsky was succeeded by Zoritch, Zoritch by Korsakov, and the latter by Lanskoy, Yermalov and Mamonov. But he, Potiomkin, continued as her inseparable companion, respected friend and adviser and sometimes as the master to whose will even the great Catherine deferred. *"J'ai un ami très capable et très digne de l'être"*, she used to say.

Most of Potiomkin's successors were completely his creatures and in his hand. Zoritch, a Serbian, might have gained some influence on Catherine's conduct of affairs of state, but he was too young. His mind was not sufficiently mature to allow him fully to realise his sudden eminence, or to exploit it to best advantage. It all happened like a dream. He had escaped from a Turkish prison in Constantinople. When he made his first appearance at Catherine's court, dressed in his close-fitting hussar's uniform, his ravishing beauty and splendid physique enchanted the Empress. He was in the flower of his youth and still possessed the unspoilt natural frankness of a young peasant. On the very first day, in addition to the customary 100,000 roubles, Catherine gave him an estate to the value of 120,000 roubles. Potiomkin was his patron; he had procured him a Captain's commission before introducing him to the Empress.

His slightest gesture sufficed to make the young Serbian's brilliant fortune, just as another wave of his hand was to cause his dazzling star to set.

Zoritch did not grace ageing Catherine's heaven for long. He was unwise enough to fall foul of his protector and challenge him to a duel. He had to go as the others before him. He, too, retained more than pleasant memories of his former position; indeed, he regained his freedom together with many advantages. His generous mistress presented him with the town of Shklov, which she elevated to a kind of principality. There, Zoritch lived like a prince in the midst of a small but lavish court. None of Catherine's lovers was taught by her to be thrifty, or was so by nature. She loved men who were recklessly lavish and generous givers and led them into such paths herself. Many a man who had learned this dangerous lesson from her later ruined himself when unable to dip into the empire's ever-filled coffers. And so Zoritch behaved. He indulged in gambling and other pleasures to excess, but could not compete with the wealth of a Potiomkin who could afford entertainments costing millions, who went from triumph to triumph and amassed ever new riches.

3. *Lanskoy*

Hardly ever did the favourite's apartments remain vacant for more than a day. After Peter Zoritch's dismissal neither the Empress nor Potiomkin had much trouble in filling the post of *vremyentchik*. The handsomest and most daring young men at court vied with each other for this honour. This time, however, Catherine's eye fell on a humbler subject. As she went for a drive one day in 1778 she noticed a sergeant of the palace guard who struck her as a paragon of physical strength and beauty. She asked who he was and learned that his name was Rimsky-Korsakov. Catherine did not hesitate to promote him to the imperial couch; the day after their first meeting he was her Adjutant-General. She liked giving nicknames to her lovers and friends and called Korsakov Pyrrhus, King of Epirus—for his beauty and the light he was spreading around her. Everything was beautiful, noble, distinguished in a man who a short while before had been drinking, cursing and swearing in the barrack room like any other sergeant; a man who had neither knowledge nor education and had yet to learn how to treat a lady. But Catherine was madly enamoured of the young man; she would not see his faults, only his virtues. Grimm failed to comprehend her taste and took this latest love of his adored empress as a passing whim, a sudden fad. Catherine was indignant at this opinion of her "souffre-douleur"; for the first time good old Grimm received a reproof from the imperial pen.

"*Engoué! engoué!* (infatuated)", she writes to him, "do you know that this is an improper term when speaking of Pyrrhus, King of Epirus? This stumbling block of painters and despair of sculptors! Nature's masterpieces, my dear sir, should inspire admiration and enthusiasm. *Des belles choses tombent et se fracassent comme des idoles devant l'arche du Seigneur.* (/other/ beauties fall and are shattered like idols before the shrine of the Lord.) Pyrrhus makes no gesture, no movement that is not noble or pleasing. He shines like the sun. He spreads light around him. Yet in all this he is by no means effeminate but completely virile and as you would want him to be. In one word: he is Pyrrhus, King of Epirus. Everything about him is in harmony: nothing is faulty in his appearance or his character. He is the sublime product of the precious gifts bestowed on him by lavish Nature. No trace of artificiality, no shadow of pretence . . ."

This paragon, however, whom she idolised was by no

means intelligent. He surpassed all his predecessors in ignorance. Shortly after his elevation to supreme office he wanted to have a library in his house in Vassieltchikov which the Empress had given him. Books, he thought, would give him a veneer of culture. He sent for a well-known Petersburg bookseller and ordered "a good library". When the bookseller asked him what kind of book he preferred the newly fledged favourite replied with great dignity: "You know best. The large books in the bottom shelves, the small ones in the upper, just as the Empress has."

He was neither faithful nor grateful. True, he was not as ungrateful as Orlov, but as he lacked Orlov's influence he could not afford to take the same liberties. Nevertheless he did, and thereby forfeited Catherine's favour. One day she surprised her beautiful Pyrrhus in the arms of a younger woman—and in her own bedroom, the love nest where she had known two years of happiness with him. Her lady in waiting and confidante, Countess Bruce, had dared to share Korsakov's love with her sovereign. Deeply shocked, Catherine hastily retreated from the room; yet the whole extent of her revenge consisted in removing both her lady and her favourite from court. Countess Bruce was sent to Moscow, and faithless Korsakov, abroad. He could have stayed with the Empress much longer, had it not been for his lapse, for he pleased her more and more. It was he who tired of her. Since neither policy nor mental affinity tied her to this man he was dismissed like a dishonest servant.

Among all the handsome men with whom Catherine whiled away the intimate hours of her life she had thus none to be particularly close to her soul, mind or heart—with the sole exception of Potiomkin. He never forgot the blissful hours when he had adored Catherine like a goddess. He remained her most loyal and trusted friend: he was not mercenary. Catherine, who knew this, preserved him her tender attachment to the end. She never changed her favourable opinion of his genius. "There is no tender endearment, my friend, that I would not say to you", she writes to him on his capture of Bender, whilst sending him a wreath of laurels made of diamonds and emeralds. At the same time, however, she warns him not to become conceited. And when he resents the suggestion she writes in her next letter: "This is what happens when one is a thousand versts apart and has to write. My heart is full of joy and has merely warned you because I wanted to spare you the one thing that could detract from the greatness of your soul." All her letters to her former lover are full of tender solicitude and sincere friendship. Occasionally she uses the familiar 'thou'. "I grab thee by the ears and kiss thee", she writes when he has taken Otchakov. The relationship between these two great people hardly betrays a change wrought by the lapse of years. Catherine allows Potiomkin to govern, to command her armies and navy, administer her provinces; she bedecks him with honours and decorations and shows him the greatest tenderness, though he has longe since been banished from the holy of holies. She calls him her disciple, her friend, her god. She praises his intellect, the nobility of his soul, his magnanimity and his heart and describes him as one of the greatest men of the century. When he neglects her she forgives him. For months on end he leaves her without news or fails to reply to her questions, especially when he rules in the Crimea as supreme commander. At last she has a letter from him, and replies, quite desperate and greatly worried over his health:

"All the time I have been without news from you I have been hanging between life and death ... For God's sake and my own, take better care of yourself than you have done. Nothing terrifies me more than to know you sick ... You are no longer a private person now, dear friend, who can live and act as he likes: you belong to the state. You belong to me."

Yes, he did belong to Russia, and to Catherine. He was her friend and not to be underestimated. She had made him a Field Marshal, Prime Minister and Prince. He possessed all honours and had all powers. When the Crimea became Russian in the course of the second Turkish war Potiomkin ruled there at will, acting as administrator and legislator, general and diplomat. Catherine gave free rein to his many-sided genius. Proudly she named him the Taurian and gave him even greater glory and riches. He became the almost sovereign ruler of the great new realm of the South.

Whenever circumstances permitted, Potiomkin would come to Petersburg, and their friendship was never shaken, though Catherine in the arms of so many unworthier men forgot that this genius was her only equal among her many lovers. The one exception was Lanskoy, who ranked next to Potiomkin in her heart. She lived with him for four blissful years, though he was only twenty-two at the time, and she, fifty-one.

On the same day Korsakov was dismissed Catherine made young Lanskoy her personal aide-de-camp. He was a poor officer in the Cavalier Guards and like most of the Empress's lovers attracted her attention through his beauty. But his beauty was not merely external, like Korsakov's; he had a noble soul and a well informed mind. His was a gentle nature: he was pleasant to everyone and had none of the haughty and brutal arrogance of some of his predecessors who abused the Empress's favour to play the tyrant. Lanskoy was kindly and humane. He was no wastrel, either, but a keen worker and a lover of the arts. His attitude towards the Empress was so unaffected and marked by such gentle courtesy that she could well believe him in love with her. What he loved most in her was her humanity and her many good qualities. Fate seems to have destined love in many forms for this woman: in her extensive love life she experienced all shades of feeling and passion. Each one of the men near her she loved in a different way, and each gave her a new and different kind of happiness. Lanskoy's golden youth shed the warmth of sunshine on her. Never did he give her grounds for displeasure. All her thoughts were for him. On him she lavished all the tender care a woman can give. He was the first whom she did not love with her senses alone; her heart, too, was his. The handsome youth might even have endangered Potiomkin's position; but the time this tenderest of lovers lived with Catherine was too short to have impaired Potiomkin's supremacy. Neither did gentle Lanskoy want it; he was not ambitious. True, his intellectual capacities would have qualified him for high office, and his lovable character would have gained him many friends and followers; but Catherine was not destined to see him as "the support of her old age", as she puts it. A sudden, unexplained death took her lover from her.

On June 19, 1784 Lanskoy fell ill while in Czarskoye-Selo with Catherine. He took to his bed with a high fever. She sent with all haste to Petersburg for her German physician, Weikard, an uncouth man but an excellent doctor who never deceived his patients or their families with evasive half-truths. The Empress, who would not move from Lanskoy's bedside, was frantic with worry. Timidly she asked the doctor what he thought of the case. "A very bad fever, Madame", replied Weikard, "he is going to die of it." Catherine was beside herself with distress. They wanted to remove her from the patient's bedside because his angina— this is supposed to have been his complaint—was considered infectious. But she did not leave him for a minute; she

LANSKOY

did not change her clothes, took hardly any food, and rendered him all the services of a devoted nurse. Yet all her love and caresses were not strong enough so save Lanskoy's life. He died in her arms ten days later, aged twenty-six.

The Empress's sorrow was heartrending. She locked herself in for several days, refused in her terrible distress to see anyone, and cried, cried. The only person she admitted was a sister of her dead lover, because she greatly resembled him.

When a week had elapsed since Lanskoy's death, Catherine began to emerge from her deep distress and tried to write to her faithful old Grimm. She took from her writing desk a letter she had begun several weeks previously, and wrote on July 2:

"When I started this letter to you I was living in joy and happiness and my thoughts were following each other so rapidly that I hardly knew whither they fled. To-day is different. I am plunged in the depths of sorrow, and my happiness has fled. I thought that I should die from the irreparable loss, a week ago, of my dearest friend. I hoped that he was going to be the support of my old age. He was attentive, he learned much, he shared my tastes and my views. I educated him; he was grateful, kind and good; he shared what sorrows I had and rejoiced in my joys. In a word, I must tell you in my tears: General Lanskoy is no more ... My room, that I had liked so well, is like a deserted cave wherein I creep about like a shadow. An inflammation of the throat seized me the day before his death, and I suffered from a burning fever. Yesterday I got up from bed, but I am so feeble and sorrowful that at present I cannot look on a human face without bursting into tears. I cannot sleep or eat. To read wearies me, writing is too much for me. I do not know what is to become of me, but I know that never in my life have I been so unhappy as when my kind, my best friend left me. 1 have opened my drawer and found this letter to you; I have written these lines—but I can do no more..."

It was only two months later that she was able to continue this sorrowful letter to Grimm. She wrote:

"I must confess I have been unable to write to you all this time because I knew we were both going to suffer. A week after I wrote to you in July I received a visit from Count Fedor Orlov and Prince Potiomkin. Until then I could not stand the sight of a human face. These two, however, knew how to approach me gently; they wept with me, and I felt better while with them. But it took me a long time to get over it; and from all this sentimentality I have become insensible of everything, except my one great sorrow. It grows stronger with every step, every word. Do not think, however, that despite my horrible depression I have displayed the slightest negligence where my attention was required. In my most terrible moments I was asked for all sorts of orders, and I gave them in an appropriate and intelligent manner. This astonished General Saltikov. More than two months passed without a change in my condition. At last I calmed down, at first for hours, then for days... Yesterday for the first time I went to Mass in Petersburg, saw people and was seen by them. But it was really too much for me. When I was back in my room I underwent such a depression as would have caused another woman to swoon... I ought to read your three letters again, but I can't... I have become a sad being that talks in monosyllables. Everything makes me sad... and yet I never liked to be an object of pity..."

Even the most censorious will forgive much to a woman who finds such words of deep sorrow and genuine feeling. Another sign of delicacy was the beautiful monument that she built for her dead lover in Czarskoe-Selo. Daily she went to that spot to shed tears of sorrow in remembrance of past happiness.

It was late in life that Catherine learned to love, but for once real love had come to her. True, she was over fifty when she met real love; before that time, deeper feelings were stifled amid the frivolity of court life. Only in middle age did she find the man who spoke to her heart rather than her senses. Her love for the youth may also have had in it some of the maternal feeling she never showed towards her own children. Perhaps she wished her own son to be like the pleasant young man she took as her lover. Soon after his death a rumour asserted that Catherine had secretly married Potiomkin. Was it gratitude, attachment or loneliness that made her take this step?—if she did take it, for there is no evidence to attest it.

4. *Potiomkin's Disgrace and Death*

A whole year passed before Catherine opened the favourite's suite to another man. Never before had it stood empty so long. Yet unfortunately, lesser men were to succeed handsome, noble Lanskoy. Fair-haired Yermalov was the ugliest, most unprepossessing and least agreeable fellow ever to attract Catherine's attention. Her choice rested between him and young Prince Dashkov, the attractive son of her old friend of revolutionary days. She may deliberately have preferred Yermalov because the Princess considered her son, who was not yet twenty, too good and too young for this post. In appointing Yermalov her Adjutant-General, the Empress was moved neither by affection nor by interest but solely by the force of habit. It is remarkable in the circumstances that he should have retained Catherine's favour for two years. He might have enjoyed it even longer, had he not incurred the Prime Minister's displeasure. Yermalov intrigued against Potiomkin where he could and managed to influence even the Empress against her great friend. In such cases Potiomkin did not waste many words; he demanded the dismissal of the obnoxious favourite. He told the Empress: "You will have to dismiss him or me. So long as you are going to keep this white nigger—" (thus Potiomkin dubbed him because of his Kalmuck cast of feature)—"I shall not set foot at court." Her attachment to Potiomkin proved stronger: Yermálov had to leave court the same day. He left with a million roubles in his pocket, and with the rank of Major-General.

It is certain that this great woman, made up of so many contrasting traits, displayed utter shamelessness in so openly and frequently changing her favourites. She showed no consideration for her exalted position nor for her womanly dignity. It is not surprising that the details of such changes furnished welcome material for gossip at court and abroad. The Empress thereby placed herself in an invidious position, and this stain on her escutcheon has prevented many biographers from rendering full justice to her many good qualities. Convention and morals were publicly flouted by her—nobody can deny it. But a character such as Catherine's, cast in a mould larger than life and holding absolute power, can easily come to disregard bourgeois morality. Strangely enough, her actions were not prompted by cynicism or a coarse lack of finer feelings, nor did she intend to challenge the conventions. Hers was not a debased nature. It seemed to her a matter of course that every Tom, Dick and Harry should be familiar with all details of her intimate life. Her own grandchildren were no strangers to her way of life; little Alexandrine, a charming young girl, and young Alexander, an idealistic youth, were often present when their grandmother left court of an evening, to disappear into her bedroom, accompanied by her current favourite.

In other respects Catherine's behaviour was serious-minded and respectable rather than frivolous. On certain occasion in her old age she did not lack some feminine modesty, her usual hearty frankness notwithstanding. One day Count Ségur, a witty and amusing companion, was sharing her coach on a journey to Kiev; he recited a poem which, though somewhat frank, was far from obscene and would not normally have offended Catherine who at her Hermitage evenings was used to much stronger fare. Ségur knew this. But on this occasion Her Majesty "was not amused": she frowned disapprovingly and brusquely changed the subject. She dismissed many courtiers who had permitted themselves improper liberties towards her ladies.

Potiomkin nominated Mamonov to replace descredited Yermalov. He, too, was a handsome and amiable young man. His reign in Catherine's inner chambers lasted three years. It was he who put an end to it, for he had more dignity than his predecessors. He always showed the greatest reverence for Catherine, now aged sixty-two; but almost from the first day since he entered her service he loved young and beautiful Princess Tcherbatov, one of the ladies at court. Mamonov was honest enough to open his heart to his mistress and ask for her consent to his marriage with the girl he loved.

Catherine had a genuine liking for Mamonov because of his many good qualities. Next to Potiomkin he was one of the most talented among her favourites. All who came near him describe him as intelligent, well informed, very entertaining and witty. He also had some artistic gifts which the Empress greatly appreciated. She called him "priceless", an "angel" who grew more lovable every day. She certainly did not like to see him go. Besides, she was jealous and bitterly offended that Mamonov should have preferred another woman to her. For months past she had sensed her lover's attachment to that lady; she suffered, but she wanted to be certain. She resorted to a stratagem. She told him—and confirmed the substance of their talk in a letter —that, as she was growing old, she wished to assure his future. She intended to marry him to a very wealthy young girl, the daughter of Count Bruce. Mamonov found himself in a dilemma. He had no choice but to confess his love for Princess Tcherbatov. "So it is true", exclaimed Catherine, deeply dejected. Later she told her intimates: "I suffered unspeakably". She could not understand that he had so long kept silence and deceived her.

Yet once again the proud woman proved generous and noble. "God be with them", she said to Potiomkin, "I have consented to their marriage; may they be happy." Yet she suffered greatly, and rumours became current at court that her sorrow over Mamonov's faithlessness had caused the Empress to show signs of mental derangement. She says in her memoirs that this was a hard lesson for her, and that she terminated the "farce" as quickly as possible. She arranged the marriage of her ex-lover to her lady-in-waiting in the most sumptuous manner, and two happy people moved to Moscow, laden with riches. As his wedding present Mamonov received 100,000 roubles, a diamond ring worth 5,000 roubles, and 2,700 peasants in the province of Nizhnij-Novgorod.

None of Catherine's friends had cause to complain of her miserliness.. According to the calculations of well-informed writers, such as the English minister, Harris, and later the historian, Castera, Catherine spent on her favourites the tremendous amount of about 450 million roubles in cash, not counting such valuables as palaces, diamonds, art treasures and serfs. Trying to justify this reckless waste she once rather cynically remarked to the Prince de Ligne: "My extravagance is really thrift. All this stays in the country and will one day come back to me." Yet she was mistaken. Many of her discarded favourites spent years abroad and there wasted their substance in orgies of spending, as did Orlov and Zubov.

Mamonov was the last favourite by the grace of Potiomkin. While he was fighting the Turks in 1789, a new young star rose in the sky. It was twenty-two years old Plato Zubov. This young man actually became a dangerous rival even to the firm friendship that bound Catherine to "little father" Potiomkin. The bonds that had for years tied her to her first minister and general were in danger of being broken by the hand of a callow youth. Potiomkin felt the danger. For the first time since Zavadovsky the Empress had not consulted her friend when choosing a new lover. He was far away. In his letters Potiomkin foamed with rage. He threatened that he was going to come to Petersburg "to have a tooth out"—a pun on the favourite's name, for *zub* means "tooth".

But although Potiomkin roared like a lion it was to no avail. His journey was long, and when the mighty man arrived, Plato Zubov had already conquered.

At first Catherine took the greatest pains to get her new protégé into her old friend's good graces. Her letters to Potiomkin during that period are full of amiable expressions, and she goes so far as to report to him the most flattering utterances about him made by her victorious lover—the "child", the "little black boy", as she calls Zubov. On one occasion she writes: "The child thinks that you are more intelligent, amusing and amiable than all those who surround you; but keep this to yourself, because he does not know that I have been told . . ."

Potiomkin, however, was not taken in. He realised the position. He knew that this "child" was going to be more powerful than all other favourites rolled into one and was not going to rest content with a cosy corner in Catherine's chamber. Zubov was even going to invade the sanctum of their friendship that Potiomkin had believed would be his forever; and the loss of Catherine's friendship would, in turn, mean the loss of his influence in matters of state. For this reason he must come to Petersburg, if all were not to be lost. In the spring of 1791 the victor of Ismaïl and Otchakov in all his glory came to his sovereign's court, thinking it an easy job to overthrow the young pretender. He gave gorgeous entertainments in his Empress's honour, unfolding all the dazzling lavishness of oriental splendour and shining in the fantastic unfolding of his extraordinary personality. At these parties Catherine was fêted more like a goddess than a mere queen. Potiomkin, lavishly squandered his immense wealth in an effect to open her eyes, to show up his rival as the mere stripling he was.

But this time he miscalculated. Catherine, though dazzled by the brilliance of her great friend, did not appear too well pleased with his presence in Petersburg just now. After one of these fêtes she intimated to Potiomkin that he must be urgently needed in the South; this entertainment she considered his farewell party. This was not so: in Prince Repnin, Potiomkin had a very efficient deputy at the front; but he had to realise with bitterness that he had played his last ace—and lost. He went—to his death.

In his absence Prince Repnin had forced the Turks to sue for peace. At any other moment Potiomkin would have been pleased, but now, considered unwanted in Petersburg, he wanted to go on making war. Full of fury, not only at his ill success in Petersburg but also at Repnin, he returned to Jassy where he had long had his headquarters and his court. He arrived, a prey to depression and unrest. He, who had never been ill, felt out of sorts. The strong man was annoyed at the thought of succumbing to illness; he would rather have fallen in battle. His impatience was boundless. While running a high fever he deliberately disobeyed his physicians' advice and ate a huge meal, consisting of salt pork, raw beets, a goose and three or four fowls, all washed down with *kvass, kluvka,* honey mead and large quantities of wine. He wanted his iron constitution to prove the stronger and refused all medicines. In his bouts of fever he had eau de cologne and ice water poured over his body; despite the hard frost he had all his windows opened and exposed himself to the rigour of the elements until even his herculean strength failed.

His death was as strange and remarkable as his life had been. Beside the road from Jassy to Nikolayev, on his way to Otchakov whither he was travelling in spite of his illness, Catherine's greatest and most gifted friend breathed his last. A sudden spasm forced the servants to lift him from the carriage to give him air. They spread his cloak at the roadside and placed the dying man on it. With him was Countess Branicka, his niece who accompanied him on all his travels. In her arms Potiomkin died.

His death left a large gap in Catherines life despite the new star lately risen in the autumn firmament of her love. Her pain was deep. She did not go out for many days and refused even to see her intimate circle at the Hermitage. Her distress made her ill. "How am I going to replace such a man?", she said to her secretary, Khrapovitsky. Now she had no one to support her, was her plaint. To Grimm she writes in the first sorrow at her irreplaceable loss: "Another frightful blow fell on my head yesterday ... My disciple, my friend and almost my god, Prince Potiomkin the Taurian, is no more ... My God, now indeed I must be Madame la Ressource: again I must educate people for my needs ... His most beautiful characteristic was the greatness of his heart, his mind, and his soul. Because of that

he was so different from all others; because of that we
were always able to understand one another and ignore
those who could not do so. I consider Prince Potiomkin a
very great man who was not allowed to do half the things
he could have done".

Yet this great woman's great weakness was love: this
is shown by the fact that in spite of all her reverence for
her dead friend she was entirely in Zubov's hands. Zubov
would not suffer mention of Potiomkin to be made in the
official Gazette; she who had been his mistress and friend
for so many years must not build him a monument nor
even erect him a modest tombstone. Zubov forbade it, and
Catherine obeyed. Legend relates that Potiomkin's body
was stolen from its tomb in St. Catherine's Church in Kherson and at the favourite's orders thrown into a ditch. What
actually happened was, however, different. Paul I ordered
the mausoleum that Countess Branicka had erected in
Kherson in Potiomkin's memory to be destroyed and his
remains to be cast away, so that no trace might remain of
the man who, while alive, had shown him much disrespect.

Much sooner, however, even in Catherine's life-time, dead
Potiomkin was forgotten. Only a few weeks after Potiomkin's death, Count Rostopchin wrote: "What is most remarkable is that he is completely forgotten. Future genera-
tions will not bless his memory. He possessed in the highest
measure the art of doing good and bad at the same time
and of incurring hatred whilst dealing out his blessings
with an open hand. It seemed as though he were resolved
to humble every man in order to rise above him."

The mighty conqueror of Tauris, decked with gold and
jewels; the founder of great cities; the man who in his person had embodied all power—he ended his life at some dusty
roadside, far from his Empress who had made him great and
powerful. And now began the reign of an insispid youngster.

CHAPTER IX

Intellectual Relationships

Voltaire and Grimm

CATHERINE'S DOMINANT characteristics were her preference for the male sex and her thirst for glory, combined with an immense vanity that ill suited a person of her genius. This boundless vanity caused her to do many things she ought not to have done: many unnecessary wars would have been avoided, much blood remained unspilled. Yet she had the satisfaction of seeing good luck and success following her every step. Her faults and blemishes have not succeeded in obscuring her greatness. Catherine will ever remain in the front rank of those whose genius, power and gifts arouse the admiration of the world. As a woman, her place in modern history is unique; there is no other woman who has achieved so much. No other woman, on the other hand, was as ambitious and vain as Catherine. She wanted to rule everywhere, not only at home but also abroad, and took good care to be an object of talk, praise and celebration. Unfortunately, she did not reject the lowest and most palpable flattery, as her friends and confidants knew full well. If someone wanted to get into the Empress's good graces the initiates would advise him: "Flatter the Empress, flatter her as much as you can, and you will succeed."

It was this vanity which brought Catherine into contact with the outstanding minds of her age. It was considered

praiseworthy to be regarded as an enlightened monarch
and to be on familiar terms with intellectual leaders. Catherine did so from the outset of her reign. Not for all
the world would she have played second fiddle in this respect to her great rival, Frederick the Great. She was, however, more generous and lavish than Frederick; she rewarded services in more royal style and therefore had a larger
retinue of flatterers. In addition, she knew how to combine
generosity with delicacy. When Diderot was in need she
bought his library and appointed him its librarian with
an annual salary of 1,000 francs. The hospitality she accorded Grimm, the offer she made to d'Alembert, to have
his encyclopedia published in Russia when its progress in
France was endangered—all these are noble traits, disclosing generosity on a grand scale. Yet here, too, an element
of vanity was not lacking. All these men were shaping
public opinion, and did not fail to praise Catherine as the
great ruler of the East, the protagonist of civilisation in
the vast realm of Russia. She loved to breathe this kind
of incense. Fully conscious of her glory, she knew how to
convey it to posterity. She once wrote to Grimm, her most
sedulous correspondent: "Fame is often the result of a
single word, a single line added at random; learned men
will search for them, lantern in hand, and stumble into
them without comprehending, if they lack sense. Ah, my
dear sir, a bushel of posthumous fame is worth all the little
glories of which you talk so much." She had no reason to
complain. The great men whose libraries or clocks she
bought or on whom she heaped other benefactions worked
hard to acquaint posterity with the fame of the "Semiramis
of the North", to convey it by the bushel by means of "a
word, a line dropped at random". In this way the ties
linking her to the free thinkers of the Occident grew ever
closer.

Catherine called herself Voltaire's disciple and his greatest admirer—as she was, in a way. We must not forget, however, that she never met Voltaire. He could never bring himself to come to Petersburg, though the Empress invited him on several occasions. This was all to the good, for personal acquaintance might have led to early estrangement. They belonged after all to different worlds. Both were egoists in regard to their fame, her egoism was tolerable only at a distance where it blended into a mutual understanding of reciprocal services and panegyrics unmarred by personal disappointment.

When Catherine first established contact with the Patriarch of Ferney she was thirty-five years old and had been Empress for eighteen months. Their relations continued in untroubled harmony to Voltaire's death fourteen years later. Catherine was a tireless letter writer. Her wealth of intelligence, wit and keen reason as well as the way in which she describes memorable happenings make her letters some of the most interesting and noteworthy documents ever penned. She voices all her thoughts with the most engaging candour and never minces matters, not even when writing to her idol, Voltaire, in whom she sees embodied the intellectual power of Europe. She was proud to be in correspondence with this Power. "It is good and useful to know such people", she writes quite frankly in the first year of their communion, thus involuntarily disclosing the selfish motives underlying this celebrated friendship. It was, indeed, very useful to her, but no less so to Voltaire. If Russia's Empress needed a pamphlet to glorify her or to convince the world of the baseness of other monarchs' actions, a courier would be sent post-haste to Ferney. He would hand the Philosopher a purse with 1,000 ducats with Her Majesty's request to name some writer suited to the task. Voltaire preferred the gold to jingle in his own pocket, and replied by return: "In order to comply with this request I have only to pocket the 1,000 ducats and dip my pen in ink". He was not only a great philosopher but also a hard-headed business man.

It is a well-known fact that under the guise of philanthropy he made his tenants manufacture clocks and watches "in order to enable them to supplement their earnings." He, however, pocketed the lion's share of these profits, for he grossly underpaid his watchmakers and workmen. He induced all his exalted patrons to buy those clocks from him. On the Empress, too, he palmed off these works of art—to the tune of 39,238 francs—by the simple expedient of sending her the lot, whereas she had ordered only some three or four thousand francs' worth in order to please him. Yet Catherine paid without demur. In return she earned bushels of fame; Voltaire was not sparing of flattery and full of praise for this noble Empress. Words did not cost much, after all: his vocabulary was well-equipped. Though he had never seen his great patroness, he found her hands to be the most beautiful in the world, her foot whiter than the snow covering her country. He called her the "Semiramis of the North", the "one great man in Europe" destined to rule the world. She has made the eighteenth century a golden age; she excels all; her mind comprehends everything; where she is, there is Paradise. She is more learned than all academies together; she dominates nature, history, nay, even philosophy. Her acts and deeds are incomparable, the greatest of the century. Her realm is unique, her laws the gospel of the world.

Here was indeed incense for Catherine—who was great enough not to have needed it. Yet she loved the intoxicating fumes of flattery. She did not know that the same Voltaire who burned incense for her wrote to his intimate friend d'Alembert: "I am entirely of your opinion that philo-

sophy can not often boast of such disciples (as Catherine).
But after all we must love our friends with all their faults."
Catherine was perhaps no more sincere when she invited
him to come to Petersburg and become a priest so that
she might be able to kiss his hand—"the hand that has
done so much good"—the Metropolitan being the only
person whose hand the Empress was supposed to kiss. One
of her letters to Grimm shows in fact that she was being
far from sincere. Both sides had been planning and seemingly longing for the philosopher's coming; but year after
year it was postponed. Whenever Voltaire wanted to come
Catherine had to visit her southern provinces or raised
some other pretext. Grimm had to be the go-between. Once,
when she seriously apprehended that Voltaire might carry
out his intention of coming to Petersburg, she wrote to
her "souffre-douleur": "Among other reasons you may
also tell him that Cato (Voltaire's name for the Empress)
is better known at a distance." This was more than a hint.
Not only she but both these gifted people feared the clash
that might destroy their mutual illusions.

Catherine learned much from the philosophers with
whom she came into contact or whose works she read;
but she utilised their ideas and principles in her own way.
Of philosophy she accepted just as much as served to her
own advantage. Thus she could afford in 1789 to say: "I
esteem philosophy, because my heart has ever been since-
rely republican." As soon as she mounted the throne, however, she ceased to be a republican, though during her reign
she introduced many reforms and gave proof of liberal
tendencies. She may have had a feeling for freedom and
the rights of man, but it remained a feeling: she was still
an autocrat. True, she freed the serfs on the ecclesiastical
estates, secularising them, much to the detriment of the
church, at the instance of a memorial which Voltaire sent

her in 1767 and which bore the motto: "*Si populus dives rex dives*"—when the people is prosperous its king is prosperous. But a short while later she wrote to Grimm: "We must admit that philosophers are queer cattle: they are born, I think, to dot all the i's and to make obscure and intricate that which is as clear as the day."

The agility of her mind was such that she viewed critically all things, including philosophy. No longer was she able to read every line written by Voltaire. The Empress who drafted her own codes of law, who was her own minister and administrator, no longer had the leisure to delve into the works of her favourite philosopher. He was too prolific an author. Catherine therefore ordered one of her secretaries to annotate every new work by Voltaire so that she might find "the reasonable and the unreasonable passages" when required. Thus prepared, the book would lie on her work desk, but only rarely did she find time to leaf through it. What she learned from other philosophers as well as Voltaire was imparted to her through correspondence, an activity she greatly enjoyed. She said she would not pass a single day without writing. Like no other sovereign, she indulged in long-winded correspondence.

When Voltaire died she bought his books for her library but even then found little time for reading, though she wrote to Grimm, who had arranged this purchase: "Will you procure me as complete an edition of his works as you can, so that I may renew and fortify my natural disposition for laughter. If you do not send them soon, you will get only elegies from me." When she wrote this, the Patriarch of Ferney had been dead only a few days. She would hardly grasp the fact that this man, "the first of his nation", was mortal. Grimm was reproached by her for not having sent her the poet's embalmed body: she would have built him a magnificent mausoleum in Petersburg. "Since Voltaire is dead", Catherine writes two months later, "it seems to me as though merriment had lost its fame. He was the god of gaiety." Another two months later she says: "I do good merely in order to do good. This has rescued me from the depression of spirit and apathy towards the things of this world with which the news of Voltaire's death had afflicted me. For he is my teacher. He, or rather his works, have formed my mind and head, as I think I have often told you. I am his pupil. When I was younger I wanted to please him. If I had done something worthy of note I had to tell him at once . . . Send me a hundred copies of the Master's works so that I can deposit them everywhere. They are to serve as an example. They are to be studied and learned by heart; I want people to enrich their souls . . ."

Catherine also wished to build a shrine in imitation of his home at Ferney: each detail was to be reproduced, down to the furniture of the room in which the great philosopher had pondered the momentous problems dealt with in his works, where he had created his masterly poetry and written his satirical novels. She would have liked to include the view of the Jura mountains in which Voltaire took such delight.

Yet how do Catherine's later actions rhyme with such outbursts of admiration? In a letter to Mamonov's father she denies nearly the whole of her correspondence with the atheist of Geneva. Though she had never prevented him from writing to her, she says, she had "never troubled to reply to him." She had rejected his advances and never entered into a correspondence with him which would have been improper for an Empress of Russia.

Thus Judas-like she denied her great master to whom, as she says herself, she owed her education. Why was this?

Because her correspondence with an atheist, if published, might have compromised her position as an autocrat and Defender of the Faith. The clergy would have been scandalised, and Catherine's relations with other European dynasties might have been imperilled, for neither she nor Voltaire minced their words when discussing other sovereigns. Catherine would call the Sultan *"le gros cochon"*, Gustavus III she derided as "Falstaff", while Frederick the Great was dubbed "Herod". In fact, she had an unkind word for everyone.

* * *

One who did not become Catherine's adulator was d'Alembert, though he was one of the first among men of letters whom she wished to distinguish. Only a few weeks after attaining the throne, in August, 1762, she wrote to the famous encyclopedist, inviting him to Petersburg. An annual salary of 10,000 roubles was awaiting him, together with permission to continue his encyclopedia which was banned in France. The only return Catherine asked of d'Alembert was to instruct Grand Duke Paul in mathematics.

But neither Catherine's incipient greatness nor the pension—which she offered to double when she learned of his reluctance—could attract the savant. He preferred his independence to the splendour of her court. D'Alembert stayed in Paris. In Petersburg, he said to his friends, people died too easily of the colic—a nasty allusion to Peter's death. Even the rank of ambassador which Catherine offered him, as well as a sumptuous house were not worth his freedom. His correspondence with the Empress lapsed and would never have been resumed, had not d'Alembert broken his silence in 1772. He begged Catherine to restore their freedom to French officers captured in Poland. He voiced this request in a very subtle manner, asking her for permission to engrave these words on his tombstone: "In the name of philosophy and humanity he obtained the freedom of French prisoners from immortal Catherine."

Catherine's reply was, however, far from amiable, and she did not release the French prisoners. In her letters to Voltaire she made fun of d'Alembert—and she could be very sarcastic. From this moment Catherine, who made so many friends, had in d'Alembert, if not an enemy, a severe critic of all her actions. Voltaire, garrulous and malicious, did not keep the Empress's mockery from his friend, and from now on d'Alembert permitted himself public criticism of her life and actions.

Yet what mattered one critic! Catherine had a veritable host of adulators, foremost among them Diderot. Their literary contact also began soon after the Empress's accession. She knew that this savant, who happened to be improvident in money matters, was in dire financial straits and besides hard hit when the encyclopedia was banned. Catherine sought at once to profit by this occasion in order to attract to her court this eminent man. He had already completed six volumes of this tremendous work and, at the age of fifty, was not the struggling beginner as described by legend. Yet at that time negotiations failed. Diderot did not want to surrender himself and his work to the unknown. Russia was a semi-barbarous country and the new Empress's throne was still shaky. Diderot had his encyclopedia printed in Neufchâtel in Switzerland, making 2,500 francs profit on each volume; in addition he had some private means. However, being not only a great spender and generous to his friends but also a gambler, he never had money, though he was not, properly speaking, a poor man. However, he was in the end compelled to think of selling his books, the tools of his trade—surely a sorry step for a savant to take. Here was an opportunity for Catherine to show her charity and generosity, and she did so in a manner worthy of the greatest praise. In 1765 she purchased Diderot's library for 15,000 francs, allowing him to keep it for life. Moreover, she appointed him librarian to his own library with an annual pension of 1,000 francs. Owing to some error payment was not made for two years. When he conveyed an indirect reminder to the Empress she made amends for her forgetfulness by paying him his pension for fifty years in advance: he got 50,000 francs and would thus have had to live to a hundred in order to work it off!

Diderot repaid her with paeans of praise. Never did Catherine have an admirer to equal him. It was then that he wrote her that celebrated letter in which he compared her to a goddess. From now on he was her most zealous servant, and Catherine had her uses for him. His knowledge of the arts was particularly useful to her. It was at Diderot's instigation that many artists and learned men came from France to Russia where they unfolded their talents and their wisdom at Catherine's court and served the great Empress. Grimm, her favourite confidant among them, owed his call to Petersburg to his friend Diderot, the Empress's commissioner. Diderot had many uses. He negotiated with Rulhière, an author who was about to publish a book on Catherine that she preferred not to see appear. He purchased valuable paintings and sculptures for her galleries, coins for her collections, selected actors and musicians for her theatres—in short, she could rely on him: he was always glad to be of service. She, in turn, did not grudge him recognition and gifts.

No wonder that the philosophers admired this universal benefactress and revered her as if she were a being of a higher order. The hearts of all these great thinkers were won by her personal charm, her unaffected style of correspondence, her brilliant mind and wit, the pleasant humour with which she derided her own class—the great ones of this world—and most of all by the marked respect she paid to leaders of thought. Even in her foreign policy Catherine appeared to these men as Iphigenia bringing civilisation to Tauris, as the protagonist of enlightenment in Poland. Even King Stanislas, though humiliated by her, shared this view.

Diderot surpassed all in his admiration for the great Empress. His heart was filled with gratitude and reverence. A tremendous plan took shape in his mind: nothing less than to begin an entire encyclopedia for the Czarina alone. It was to be a kind of supplement to the thirty volumes then in preparation, a dictionary of philosophy that was to comprise the world's thinking in its entirety and was intended to be a useful compendium for his wise sovereign and her successors. Although he had by now reached the age of sixty he did not recoil from this giant labour: for Catherine he felt able to do anything.

Now it was he who suggested that he should come to Petersburg in order to devote to her alone the last years of his creative life. His friend Falconet who spent some time at the court of Petersburg submitted this plan to the Empress. At first she hesitated to call Diderot, for at that time she was fully occupied with foreign policy. The Turkish war demanded all her attention and energy. In the end, Diderot was permitted to come to Russia's capital, this time in an official capacity: as ambassador in charge of a mission from Catherine's new ally, France. On his way to Russia he was however more occupied with his own ideas and plans. His head was full of large projects, and he was convinced that the Empress's "blessed hand" would gladly seize the opportunity of furthering the giant work

he was going to give to the world. He imagined the joy
with which Catherine was going to receive him, the missionary who was bringing Europe's new thoughts to semi-
barbarous Russia.

Yet Diderots first days in Petersburg brought him some
disappointment. Neither did he see the Empress, nor had
she provided accommodation for him. Leon Narishkin
looked after him and opened him his hospitable house. The
time of Diderot's arrival was ill-chosen. People were full
of other things and had no time for scientific and literary
plans. Petersburg resounded with gorgeous fêtes. Grand
Duke Paul had married Princess Maria Feodorovna of
Hesse-Darmstadt. A new favourite had moved into Catherine's apartments, and at that moment—towards the end
of 1773—she was absorbed in waging war. Rumiantsov was
fighting under the walls of Silistria, while on the banks of
the river Jaik Pugatchev's famous rebellion was raging.
Catherine's hands were thus full.

Her universal mind, capable of doing a hundred things
at once, did not forget the philosopher, her greatest admirer
who had hastened to her from the West. The portals of the
palace opened to Diderot, and in the end Catherine received
him daily in confidential audience. They would sometimes
spend three hours in lively conversation. Despite his sixty
years Diderot was still a firebrand, a true son of his country who gesticulated while talking. When in the heat of
talk he thought the Empress lacking in proper appreciation
of his maxims he would bang the table with his fist or
excitedly run up and down the room, waving his arms. In
such moments of intimacy most of Catherine's interlocutors
were apt to forget that they were in the presence of an
Empress to whom observance of etiquette was due. Her
mind in such talks was so human, so unaffected and keen
that the greatest thinkers accepted her as their equal. Dide-

rot's conversations with her show to what extent people could let themselves go when talking with Catherine. "He takes her by the hands, shakes her by the arm, bangs the table as though he were in Holbach's house in the Rue Royale", writes Grimm.—And what did Catherine have to say to her high-spirited guest? She smiled, and with a delicious sense of humour wrote to Madame Geoffrin "that she was compelled to interpose a table between herself and Diderot in order to have some degree of protection from his expressive gestures, for her knees and arms were already black and blue."

Yet despite this familiarity Diderot's talks with Catherine had no positive result. The new encyclopedia was not discussed: it failed to materialise. Neither was philosophy the gainer. Diderot's extraordinary eloquence had no influence on the woman who had plotted her own course and followed only her own plans, her own genius. She let Diderot talk, argued with him, but her masculine intellect was not to be sidetracked for a moment. The deed, not the word influenced Catherine. Eloquent herself, she remained unconvinced by the eloquence of others. The philosopher's ideas on social reforms were not hers. She would fail to reply to his earnest, searching questions, or turn them aside with some witty quip or, sometimes, a correction. When he inquired one day about the living conditions of the "slaves" that were, regrettably, still to be found in her realm, she retorted severely that he was employing a term not only improper but banned in Russia. There were no slaves in her country but only "people tied to the soil they cultivate." She seemed to forget that in her own instructions to the legislative commission she had used the term "slave".

Neither of them was fully satisfied with the other, though they tried to give that appearance. The Empress

did not seem to consider Diderot suitable for the mission
with which he had been charged. She thought him partly too
old, partly too young. "In some respects", she said to Ambassador Durand, "he gives the impression of being a hundred
years old, while in other respects he acts like a ten-year old."
Diderot on the other hand was disappointed that none of
his plans had found favour, none of his ideas had taken
root. Yet before the world he sang the Empress's praises.
She had assured his future; he owed her that. Without
being conscious of the fact he had entered upon the slippery
slope of the courtier who shrinks from no degree of flattery. Catherine often ridiculed him with the downright
frankness she affected. One day he was speaking of the
horrible fate that must be in store for courtiers who had
spent their lives in fawning upon their princes. If there
was a purgatory, a special corner must surely be set aside
for them to roast on the spit. It was meant as a pleasantry,
but Catherine's face became suddenly serious and thoughtful. Abruptly she asked him: "What do they think in Paris
about my husband's death?" Diderot almost fell from his
chair at this question and was at a loss what to say. He
tried to extricate himself like an accomplished courtier
and began to talk of the hard tasks demanded from those
who sat on the throne. Greatness of soul was what was
expected of them, and so on. Catherine interrupted him
and said laughing: "It seems to me, Monsieur Diderot,
you are heading straight for Purgatory." He had had his
lesson.

His stay at Catherine's court was coming to an end.
In the spring of 1774 he took his leave from his great
friend who, despite their intimacy, did not lavish laurels
or riches upon him. His character was too noble for that;
he was too much the artist, too little a business man. Unlike
others, he had been incapable of exploiting the treasures

and the generosity of his exalted patroness. Their relations
had in the end assumed a footing of equality. He behaved
like a grandee towards a highly-placed lady and felt obliged
to make her presents far in excess of his means and which
greatly reduced the amounts Catherine's generosity had
granted him. He wrote to his wife what he did not wish
to say in public: "On the eve of my departure from Petersburg Her Majesty sent me three bags containing 1,000
roubles each... If I deduct from this sum what I paid
for an enamel plaque and two paintings which I presented
to the Empress, as well as the expenses of my return
journey and the presents which decency compels us to
give to the Narishkins . . . some five to six thousand
francs are left, perhaps even less."

Diderot forgot a few little items. Not only had he been
living for six months at the Empress's expense, but he
had also received his life pension of 50,000 francs in advance; in addition, he had drawn some 12,000 francs for
incidental expenses from the Privy Purse, not counting the
many presents Catherine had made him. True, here was
no wealth beyond the dreams of avarice, especially as he
realised that he could have had much greater rewards, had
he so desired. In order not to lay himself open to the ridi-
cule of his friends he wrote to Mile. Volland: "I return
from Petersburg loaded with honours. If I had wanted to
dip freely into the Imperial coffers I could have done so.
But I preferred to silence the gossips of Petersburg. By
Heaven, you can believe everything I am going to say about
that extraordinary woman. My praise is not paid. . . All the
thoughts that filled my mind when I left Paris vanished
in the first night I spent in Petersburg..."

This one sentence says everything. It is expressive of
Diderot's disappointment over his sojourn at the court of
Petersburg. Yet he still cherished hopes that the greatest

queen ever to sit on a throne was going to realise his ideas
and execute his plans. As soon as he was back in Paris the
thoughts that had left him in Russia returned. His praise,
his enthusiasm for Catherine redoubled. Entire pages in
his correspondence with her are devoted to admiration of
her unique genius. In her, "the soul of Brutus was united
to the charms of Cleopatra." On his return to Paris he
was of course besieged on all sides: people wanted to know
the least detail about the Empress and her character.
Proudly he reports to her how he answered these questions.
"Your Majesty's talents and virtues have become the subject of our evening parties. They want to know everything:
she has a most noble face?—None nobler. You say she is
extremely charming and amiable?—Anyone who knows her
will say the same. You did not tremble when you came
before her?—I beg your pardon, my trembling did not last
long; for when one is with her one thinks neither of her
high rank nor her greatness; in the twinkling of an eye she
makes you forget all that. Does she possess firmness?—
She told me herself that she is at her best in moments of
peril. Does she love the truth?—She loves truth as much
as I condemn those who dare not tell her the truth. Is
she well-informed?—She is better informed about her immense empire than you are about your small domestic affairs."

What woman would not have felt flattered by such
praise? Catherine showed herself grateful, though in a
different way than Diderot had expected. Though she did
not, as he had hoped, put at his disposal the 200,000 francs
necessary for the compilation of his new encyclopedia, she
helped him out with smaller sums which the philosopher,
always short of money, needed for his living expenses. In
this she gave proof of great kindness of heart. In 1784,
when the old man was suffering from asthma and was no

CATHERINE THE GREAT

longer able to climb the four flights of stairs to his apartment in the Rue de la Vieille Estrapade where he had been living for thirty years, she rented for him a more convenient apartment in the Rue Richelieu. Yet he was not to enjoy this gift from his benefactress for long. Barely a fortnight later he choked to death. Catherine's letters to Diderot have unfortunately fallen victim to the storm of the revolution. His daughter, Madame de Vandeuil, destroyed them when fearing a domiciliary search in 1792.

* *
*

Even before Diderot saw the splendour of the Russian court, the most Frenchified of Germans, Baron Grimm, had become friendly with this most Germanised of Frenchmen. Largely because of this friendship he became Catherine's closest spiritual confidant. To no one did she show herself so unaffected, so completely human as to Grimm. Her correspondence with him fills two thick tomes and extends over a period of twenty years. How many letters of this interesting correspondence may yet lie hidden in the secret archives of Petersburg! How many, too, may have been lost! Mental communion with Grimm became her indispensable habit. She wrote to him whenever she could, her letters having the character of a diary. Little allusion is made to politics in these letters during the earlier period; it is only after 1787 that political happenings find more frequent mention. The time of the French Revolution plays an important part in these masterpieces of the art of letter-writing.

Catherine made Grimm's acquaintance through his literary newsletter, the "Correspondance littéraire", which he sent to most German and some foreign courts. Ever since 1764 the Empress of Russia was one of his first subscribers, and a generous one, for she paid 1,500 roubles a year while Frederick the Great paid nothing, and King Stanislas of Poland a mere 400 francs a year. In the course of time Grimm, always well-informed in matters literary and artistic, emerged as Catherine's useful man of all work—her factotum, as he used to describe himself. The close friendship, however, that actually bound them to each other dates only from 1773.

About this time Grimm came to the court of Petersburg in the entourage of the landgravine whose daughter Grand Duke Paul married. He made a good impression on Catherine, but she did not yet retain him at her court. He had no inclination to settle in Petersburg, for he loved Paris above everything. But there he intended to devote himself completely to the Russian Empress's service, the more so as she had given him permission to write to her directly, a favour enjoyed by only a selected few. With great skill Grimm soon managed to become indispensable to her, partly by virtue of his intellect and his truly eminent talents in many fields, but not the least also by means of excessive flattery. When he first came to Petersburg he had long ceased to be the poor devil whom Rousseau had known as Count Friesen's secretary. Sainte-Beuve used to call him "Minister Resident and Plenipotentiary of the Powers at the Court of French public opinion and esprit." He was at the same time the missionary of the French spirit and French civilisation among the European Powers. Unfortunately he became proud and conceited when he had become the owner of medals and decorations and lost his natural simplicity. This learned man was a great flatterer, too, and often indulged in abject fawning before the Empress. Catherine could stand flattery in large doses, but this lickspittle behaviour or her "souffre-douleur", whom she preferred less affected, occasionally became too much for her. She laughed at him and ridiculed him; but he waxed only more senti-

mental, more lyrical, and his affectation was manifest. When
he receives a letter from her he wants to rush to his immortal mistress, to kiss her knees and bathe them in tears
of joy and gratitude. His eyes become springs, and he dis-
solves in tears; a thousand times he kisses the sacred
letters, written by her august hand; he would expire with
grateful emotion. He even forgets all dignity and begs her
"to count him among her dogs."

This man was very useful to Catherine, and she culti-
vated his friendship. He was her agent in Western Europe.
He held large sums of money in her behalf, bought pictures and other works of art, maps, books, travel guides;
he paid pensions to many poor artists, writers and royalists
supported by her, and was ever ready to advise her. Catherine was also very fond of chatty correspondence, and no
one was better suited for this than Grimm. She was very
grateful for the sympathetic way in which he reacted to
her long letters and claimed that no one understood her
better. She dubbed him "souffre-douleur" (long-suffering)
because of the way she bombarded him with her letters.
She was wont to give such nicknames to everyone who
came near her. Herself she calls "garrulous". "We are
inveterate gossips", she writes on one occasion, "but scrib-
bling happens to be my vocation ... I believe we were both
made to live pen in hand, sending each other interminable
letters." On another occasion she writes: "You don't have
to read my letters; throw them into the fire if you like."
In general she likes to joke about their correspondence.
"When you marry," she jokes, "you can keep your spouse
in curl-papers for a long time to come: you need but use
these beautiful letters". The entire correspondence is per-
vaded with a delightful sense of humour. She was happy
to be able to behave in a completely natural manner before
Grimm, whereas towards Voltaire whom she regarded as

the intellectual leader of his age, she felt constrained to be on her guard. With Grimm much more than with Voltaire she pokes fun at the great ones of this world. "Do you know why I am afraid of royal visitors?", she asks, and replies herself: "Because they are usually dull and boring, and you have to be all stiff and correct with them. Even famous people appreciate my artlessness; I want to be witty 'comme quatre', yet often I have to be witty 'for four' in order to be able to listen to them. Being garrulous myself I feel bored when I have to remain silent." She would often poke fun at Grimm himself. At times she would address him by the familiar 'thou' or give him humorous nicknames such as *"Monsieur le hérétique"*, *"Georges Dandin"*, *"Monsieur le Freiherr"*, *"Heraclitus"*, *"Monsieur le philosophe"*. Her letters are full of bubbling humour and gaiety.

When Grimm came to Petersburg in 1776 in order to attend Paul's second marriage he was persona grata. Catherine chattered with him for hours on end, and these protracted "audiences" did not fail to arouse the attention and jealousy of foreign diplomats. Grimm had become a personage, but he did not abuse his prominence. He refused all the high offices in Russia that Catherine offered him. When he left Petersburg in August, 1777 after a year's stay the Empress granted him an annual pension of 2,000 roubles. When he subsequently lost a large part of his fortune and his income owing to the Revolution she made him several money gifts, totalling 60,000 roubles.

Following Grimm's second visit to Petersburg his friendship with the Empress became closer and their correspondence even more frequent. Both were delighted with each other. Catherine could have made her friend a minister, but Grimm wanted to be no more than her factotum, her *"souffre-douleur"*. And that is what he was. On him she could devolve all her cares and worries; with him she could talk about all her affairs, both of state and heart. Conscientiously she would inform him of every change in her inner chamber, discuss all her plans with him. She conceived her plans and ideas on a grand scale and would then discuss their general outline in her free and easy way. At other times she vented her anger over some weakness, untruth, stupidity or indecision shown by other monarchs. Even kings were not spared her caustic criticism. Of Gustavus III of Sweden she once said: "Here is a king who thinks to acquire much glory by cheating and lying, but he is going to be the butt and shame of posterity: lying and cheating does not lead to honour and glory." She would criticise other crowned heads in her quaint old-fashioned German: *"Was aber anbelangt die ehrwürdige Frau Betschwester, so kann ich von ihr anders nichts sagen, als dass sie grosse Anfechtungen der Hab- und Herrschsucht leidet."*—(As regards that snivelling bigot [Empress Maria Theresia of Austria who cried over the fate of Poland] I must say that she suffers from great temptations of avarice and lust for domination). She goes on to say: "Her blubbering may be evidence of repentance, but as she goes on grabbing and keeping things she seems to forget that this is no true repentance. There must be some obduracy in her yet; I fear me that old Adam's original sin causes her to play such a wicked comedy. But what more is asked of a woman", adds Catherine, ironically alluding to her own damaged reputation, "than to remain faithful to her husband: if she does that she has all the virtues, and nothing more is expected of her." Maria's son, Joseph II, comes in for his mead of censure. She calls him "Herr Janus, of whom one may predict without fear of error that, should he fail to become a great man, he will be very much annoyed and take it out of others for what he lacks in appearance, soul and mind." On another occasion, while admitting his talents, she says of him: "I can not get over my amazement that he, bred, born and trained for his dignity and so full of wit, talents and knowledge, should rule so badly and unsuccessfully."

Common sense dictates most of her judgments. She is a realist, putting its proper value on a thing and, though sometimes mistaken, never accepting mere words in lieu of ideas. Only where love enters into her scheme of things does Catherine lack her customary clear-sightedness. Rarely was her policy influenced by personal considerations, however closely politics and love may have walked together in her life. She had her own ideas and views on everything. Whether it is politics, religion, literature, art, philosophy, education or people and everyday matters that she discusses with her correspondents, especially Grimm—Catherine is always herself and never belies her individuality. Her views on music and painting, wherein she was utterly ignorant, are not always correct but always her own. Her style, too, her choice of expression and her behaviour is completely original. But all this is dominated by her delightful sense of humour, her gay and carefree nature, and the profundity of her all-embracing genius.

No wonder that in the twenty-seven years of their friendship Grimm was completely bound up with the woman whose personality was much stronger than his and who in the end absorbed him altogether. As an old man, shortly before his death, he wrote: "This correspondence has become the sole blessing and ornament of my life, the main prop of my fortunes and so essential to my life that it seems more needful than drawing my breath ... Far from her, I had in the end established a sort of cult, devoted only to veneration of her. The thought of her had taken such root in me that it left me neither by day nor by night and all my ideas centred in it . . . Whether I walked or travelled, sat or lay or stood—my being had completely fused into hers." He lived and thought only in her. Shortly before his death Catherine appointed him Russian Minister-Resident in Hamburg, and Paul I confirmed his mother's friend in his office.

Grimm was a true friend. Catherine had no servant and adviser more faithful, devoted and honest. She never had to fear his indiscretion; he was almost alone among her many admirers and friends in never abusing her favour. Her death left a large gap in his life. Though six years older than Catherine, he survived her by eleven years and died at Gotha at the age of eighty-four.

CHAPTER X

Work and Relaxation

CATHERINE'S PRIVATE LIFE is usually depicted in glaring colours. The Empress is represented as having indulged in daily orgies of the grossest kind in the company of abandoned men and women. The palaces of Petersburg, Czarskoe-Selo, Oranienbaum and especially the Hermitage are described as nests of licentiousness and moral corruption, with Catherine as the worst offender.

Yet when we scrutinise more closely the life of this extraordinary woman we find that it appears much less amoral than legend, calumny and gossip have related. True, the harmonious belance in her character and mode of life, the strict regularity of her extensive labours, her leisure and amusements contrast sharply with her intimate life; but they also enable us to cast a veil of indulgence over a woman of genius who felt entitled to greater latitude than others of her sex. Catherine, admittedly, was insatiable both in love and ambition; but her voluptuousness as well as her ambitions were kept within certain limits which she rarely transgressed. She never lost herself in either. Her lovers occupied a large place in her life and her palaces and often had a pernicious influence on the economic, political and moral welfare of the state, but Catherine always maintained her dignity as Empress and as a woman. She was, indeed, a womanly woman, the soul of her household, her family, her court and her social circle. Her private life was as simple and unostentatious as the luxury and pomp she showed to the outside world. She disliked having a multitude of servants around her; two or three who were really reliable were sufficient. She preferred doing things for herself: in this way the ever active woman lost less time. She treated all her subordinates with the greatest kindness. She did not command, she asked for a service, even of the youngest footman, and the word "please" was never absent from her orders. As she was somewhat short-tempered it would happen that she flared up when someone interrupted her at work or when writing, and then some hard word might escape her. The next moment found her sorry, and she tried to make amends for her temper by apologising. "Will I ever manage not to be feared?", she said with regard to her domestics. Her indulgence at times went too far so that ungrateful people abused her kindness, but her servants on the whole loved and revered her and would have gone through fire and water for her.

Catherine's work started at an early hour. She usually got up at six in the morning. At first her consideration for her staff went so far that she made a fire and lighted candles herself so as not to wake the tired servants at that early hour. In later years she changed her habits, not because she thought these small domestic chores beneath her, but because her time was too valuable. For the same reason she held only a small levee, usually around one o'clock in the afternoon, attended by a few friends and some high dignitaries. Until then, she worked either alone or with her secretaries, received ministers, generals and diplomats, savants and artists, and even found time for an intimate tête-à-tête with the favourite of the moment.

Her bedroom in the Winter Palace was adjoined by her official dressing room and in addition by a smaller private room where she made her first, perfunctory toilet. She required only one maid for minor attentions. The Empress got up, washed her face with ice water, rinsed her mouth with lukewarm water and donned a voluminous pleated morning robe of white flannel. A little Kalmuck girl who was always with her quickly dressed her hair and crowned it with a white frieze boudoir cap—the same mob-cap which Grimm relates she used to push from one ear to the other in the heat of conversation. This rapid toilet took barely ten minutes but for the time being satisfied the Empress. Then she walked rapidly into her study, followed by her five pet dogs who spent the night by her bed, sleeping in a basket of pink silk and lace.

Before Catherine sat down at her desk she drank several cups of extremely strong coffee. Her cook used one pound of coffee for five cups, and rarely did she fail to empty them. Anybody else would have had heart trouble, drinking this powerful decoction, but Catherine needed the stimulant.

Until nine o'clock the Empress remained alone in her study, immersed in her correspondence or engaged on other work. We know that she was a great letter-writer. Even though most of her letters were taken down by three or four secretaries there were many which she wrote with her own hand, as for instance almost the whole of her correspondence with Grimm, and the letters to Voltaire which she copied out after they had been drafted on her instructions. While at work Catherine constantly took snuff, even when young. At that time it was not thought unwomanly or unbecoming for a pretty young woman to take a pinch of snuff, just as nowadays it is no longer considered objectionable for ladies to smoke.

At the stroke of nine the Empress rose from her desk and returned to her bedroom. Here she received high officials making their reports, generals and ministers who had requested an audience, and her private secretary to whom she gave instructions. He was the first to be called in. Catherine graciously extended her hand which he kissed reverently; then he was invited to sit down at a desk where he awaited her orders. His work was often interrupted, for at frequent intervals ministers, high officials and officers were announced, all of whom she received with gracious dignity. The eyes of all these courtiers, young and old, shone with boundless admiration for her genius and reverence for her power. General Suvorov adored his revered sovereign to the point of idolatry. After making the sign of the cross and genuflecting before all the ikons in the room he also crossed himself before Catherine, though she sat before him, not with crown and sceptre nor a halo around her head, but as an ordinary mortal in a dressing gown, her mob-cap a little crooked over one ear. This did not prevent the fanatic from kneeling before her, as to a saint. She would reprove him for his crazy behaviour, and then rapidly question him on the latest military intelligence. Then it was someone else's turn, then another and yet another. All at once the chamberlain on duty approached the Empress and mysteriously whispered into her ear what everybody knew. At a gesture from Catherine everybody left the room: the favourite was coming. He had the privilege of admission at all times and could visit the Empress even while at work. In fact, she liked these official attentions; she wanted people to see that she was all woman, and still desirable. She wanted them to say: "Her Majesty has just received the favourite." He did not usually remain with her longer than half an hour; when he had gone she continued working with her secretaries until noon or one o'clock. At that time Catherine dismissed her secretary and went to her private dressing room where Kotzlov, her hairdresser, was waiting for her.

Even in her old age she still had a beautiful head of hair. Her tresses were long and thick, and when she sat at her dressing table it hung to the ground in soft, silky waves. It was always beautifully kept: she wore it swept off her face, thus displaying her high and thoughtful brow. She now exchanged her white morning dress for a grey or purple silk gown of loose and simple style and devoid of ornament. On ordinary occasions she wore neither jewelry nor decorations. Her tiny feet were encased in open low-heeled shoes, thus running counter to the contemporary fashion of very high-heeled footwear. Catherine was not coquettish in her dress and all reports agree that she always dressed in perfect good taste. Even in later years, when she grew excessively stout, she wore well-cut garments that succeeded in disguising the faults of her figure.

When Catherine had completed her toilet she adjourned to the official dressing room where she held her levee, whilst four maids put on the finishing touches at a sumptuous dressing table made of pure gold. Of pure gold, too, were the basin into which she dipped her fingers and the casket with hairpins which a maid tendered to her. In the meantime the medium-sized room filled with courtiers honoured with an invitation to the Empress's levee. She was completely natural, vivacious, amiable, spirited and witty. She looked fresh and well-groomed as her intelligent grey eyes roved from one guest to another. None of those present was embarrassed or overpowered by the exalted presence. Her friendly behaviour created a pleasant atmosphere. She would laugh at Leon Narishkin's quips or the antics of her female buffoon, Matrena Danilevna. Catherine was particularly fond of her because Matrena was the faithful reporter of all court news and gossip. Like many great rulers, Catherine loved to listen to gossip, though merely for her private amusement.

The principal actor at the imperial levee was, however, the favourite, whether his name be Lanskoy, Mamonov or Zubov, and of course all-powerful Potiomkin, unless his duties as a general kept him from court. When Catherine's grandchildren reached a certain age they too could come to their grandmother's levee.

At one o'clock—later at two—Catherine sat down at table. Only a few people had the honour of dining with the Empress. The favourite would sit at her right hand. In earlier years her intimate friends were invited to table. among them Princess Catherine Romanovna Dashkov; Countess Bruce, the lady-in-waiting; Potiomkin's niece, Countess Branicka; the two Narishkin brothers; Field-Marshal Prince Galitzin; Prince Potiomkin; Count Chernitchev; Count Stroganov; Prince Bariatinsky; the Orlovs and Count Razumovsky. Some of these persons later dropped out and were replaced by others, such as Demoiselle Protasov, Vice-Admiral Ribas, young Bobrinsky's tutor, and several others.

Catherine was no epicure; the food at her table was indifferent. For years she kept a cook whom Brillat-Savarin would not have tolerated in the lowest eating-place of the Paris boulevards. Catherine did not even notice that he was a bad cook. When her attention was finally drawn to this fact, she could not make up her mind to dismiss him, as he had been in her service such a long time. When he was on duty and sent in dishes that were hardly eatable the Empress merely laughed and remarked: "Ladies and gentlemen, it seems Lenten week is here again." However, her ladies and gentlemen recouped themselves elsewhere; for even though Catherine spent comparatively little on her table, Nikolai Saltikov, Branicka, Potiomkin and Zubov dipped sufficiently into the imperial coffers not to miss any of the pleasures of the table. For their table alone,

Potiomkin and Zubov needed 400 roubles a day, not counting another 200 roubles for wine, coffee, tea and chocolate —all this for one day's food!

Dinner was followed by some conversation; then the Empress dismissed her small party and retired to her boudoir with her embroidery. She loved to do some embroidering, sewing or knitting while Betzky, her mother's mysterious friend in Paris and Catherine's alleged father, read to her from her favourite authors. When Betzky grew too old she read herself. In time, however, Catherine's eyes, too, grew weaker and she had to wear spectacles. She only needed them for reading and did not require them for writing, but this sign of old age annoyed her. One day, when her secretary, Khrapovitsky, was in the room and saw her putting on her glasses in order to decipher some document, she said to him, jokingly: "You don't need that sort of thing, what? How old are you?"—"Twenty-six, Your Majesty."—"Oh, then you have not had time to spoil your eyes in the service of the state as I have done."

In these hours of repose—often interrupted by business, for one of her secretaries was always in attendance—she would often send for children and played with them in the intervals of business or conversation. In later years her grandchildren would come and play in her room. Though she had not much fondness for her own son she adored children. Some of her young favourites, such as little Markov and the son of Admiral Ribeaupierre, she had brought up at court. The children of Prince Galitzin, four young nephews of Potiomkin, the son of Count Nikolai Saltikov, little Count Valentine Esterhazy, a child of Count Shuvalov's—all of them were allowed to play in Catherine's apartments, and she romped with them like any child. When she was younger there would be great tumblings on the floor; the high spirits of the children were equalled

by those of the Empress, Gregory Orlov and Zachar Chernitchev. Later, when Catherine's growing stoutness prevented her from rolling on the carpet with the little ones
she cut out paper dolls for them, made them toys of card-
board and paper, drew cartoons for them and told them
fairy tales or funny stories so that the merry laughter of
children was ever about her. She loved it, as she loved
gaiety, youth and everything simple. Next to children,
Catherine was fond of animals. She was always surrounded
by a large dog family; in her letters to Grimm and others
the famous "Family Anderson" plays no mean part. In
her amusing manner she chatted charmingly about the
"Andersons"; on one occasion she wrote:

"Chief of the clan is Sir Tom Anderson; his consort is
Lady Anderson, and then there are their offspring: young
Lady Anderson, Monsieur Anderson and Tom Anderson.
The last-named lives in Moscow under the guardianship of
Prince Volkonsky, Governor-General of that city. In addition to Tom, whose reputation is established, there are
four or five young 'people' of promise who are being
brought up in some of the best houses in Moscow and Petersburg, such as those of Prince Orlov, Monsieur Narishkin or Prince Tufiakin. Sir Tom Anderson has contracted
a second marriage with Miss Mimi who is now called Mimi
Anderson; but there is not as yet any progeny. Apart from
this legitimate union (for history is bound to mention
peoples' failings as well as their virtues) Monsieur Tom
has had several extra-marital relations. The Grand Duchess
[Paul's wife] has a number of pretty bitches who have
turned his head, but no bastard has so far been born to
him, and it seems there are not going to be any. This shows
that, whatever people may say, it is pure calumny."

Catherine would remain in her salon until four o'clock,
busied with her work or with the children. From then on

until six she adjourned to the Hermitage together with her favourite. It was her dearest retreat, where everything was furnished to her taste. From these cosy, artistically furnished rooms she had banished etiquette. Here people could be human. Catherine needed this relaxation, the free and easy behaviour that sometimes bordered on coarseness.

The Hermitage occupied an entire wing of the Petersburg Palace. A large part of it was formed by a very valuable and comprehensive picture gallery and the priceless collection of *objets d'art* and books which Catherine's excellent taste had brought together. There were also two large card-rooms and a dining room where intimate little supper parties sat around two medium-sized tables. Adjoining these rooms was a magnificent conservatory with the rarest plants and flowers. People walked under tropical trees and among exotic plants as if in fairyland: birds of gorgeous plumage sang their sweetest songs, and at night a magic light filled the enchanted space.

Most pleasant of all was the unrestricted freedom that prevailed in these private apartments. A large placard at the entrance of this retreat set the tone that was demanded of the entrant. It said: "It is forbidden to get up when the Empress comes in, even when you are sitting and see her approaching you, or if she wishes to remain standing while addressing you. It is further forbidden to show bad temper, to exchange insults, to speak ill of others or to remember any disputes or differences with another guest which one might have in the outside world: they are to be left in the cloakroom together with your hat and stick. Lying and fibbing are also prohibited." Any infringement of these rules was punished with a fine of ten kopecks, to be put in the poor box; takings were never small. Bezhborodko acted as cashier. The evening usually concluded with a rubber of whist. It happened that a player would throw his cards on the table in a fury because his imperial partner had trumped his ace. This even happened at official card parties at court. Tchertkov, a gentleman of the bedchamber, often flew into a fury when playing cards with the Empress. One night he brusquely rose from the gaming table, threw his cards on the floor and claimed that the Empress had cheated. Catherine, by no means offended, defended herself and called the other players to witness.

Only a small number of chosen guests were received by Catherine in her secluded Hermitage. Neither Versailles nor Trianon heard what the walls of her private rooms in Petersburg witnessed in the course of the Empress's evening parties. Some of the jokes made there were so ribald that even a man of the world like Count Ségur felt embarrassed, whilst Catherine was fit to burst with laughter and roared till her ribs ached. Leon Narishkin set the tone: he was full of ever new quips and sallies that greatly amused Her Majesty. Harmless parlour tricks were also popular: the great Empress was extremely proud of being able to waggle her right ear without distorting her face. Baron Vanyura, on the other hand, was much envied and caused endless amusement by being able to waggle his wig. Another game was forfeits. It often happened that when the pledges were redeemed the Empress was made to sit on the floor: and she did, though not without difficulty, for she was very stout. Everybody laughed at the comical figure she cut in doing so. Or she had to empty a glass of water in one gulp, or recite a passage from Trediakovky "Telemachiad" without yawning. Doggerel rhymes were made on this or that member of the party, and the Empress proved particularly adept in this kind of "poetry". Once she made the following verses on her dear Narishkin:

For the Information of Posterity
An Inscription
To be Placed on the Foundation-Stone of the Country House
of Leon Narishkin, Grand Master of the Horse.
"Behold the House of Sir Leon Narishkin, Grand Master
of the Horse".

Of him no horse had reason to complain
For never did he hold the horseman's rein.
To him as babe Dame Nature promised beauty,
Yet when he grew seem'd to forsake her duty.
When he would wed he took to him for wife
A maid he'd never seen in all his life.
Though liking wine and women and fine clothes
He was not drunk, in love, or wiped his nose.
Of barbers, lest they scar him, was he scared,
Yet he was cut when he at Court appeared.
He crav'd for tender dalliance, but found none:
When he waxed bold, the frighted nymph was gone.
A nimble dancer he, who skipp'd about —
Or would have, if he had not been too stout;
A wealthy man, yet penniless, who sought
To purchase all those things he needed not.
Of all his treasures he lov'd best, I trow,
The little plot where you are standing now.
Here every year our Leon could be seen
Planting his pleasaunce with much boscage green.
Eke had he fountains, and a brook withal
That stopp't its course when rain refused to fall.
His motto was: Be, and make others, gay.
He liked to gambol (gamble, too!) and play:
In joy and laughter did he spend his day.

These were the more harmless amusements of the Hermitage. Completely different, however, were the hours she
would spend there of an afternoon with her favourite. With
him—especially in the days of Lanskoy and Potiomkin—
she would inspect new works of art for her collection, or
have it rearranged; browse among new books that had
arrived for her library; or else she would play a game of
billiards with her favoured companion. These hours of the
day Catherine liked best. But at the stroke of six she had
to tear herself away from this almost bourgeois existence.
The time for the official dinner and reception had arrived.

The Empress once again returned to her private chambers in order to adjust her dress, for she changed it only
on very special occasions for evening court. At such times
she would don full court dress, usually a dark red velours
gown of Russian style. Her luxuriant hair was topped by
a diamond-studded crown—and no head was more fit to
wear a crown than Catherine's with its wise and majestic
countenance. Yet it seemed as though she changed her
character with her clothes when putting on her court dress.
As soon as she had donned her long gloves and appeared in
the reception halls she was no longer the gay, merry woman
with her little human weaknesses: now she was the sovereign, majestic and dignified, gracious and condescending.
Though short rather than tall, she was impressive; she
carried herself well, her head held high but her mien friendly and amiable. Slowly, with short, measured steps she
walked between the rows of courtiers who bowed to the
ground, saluting them with a slight, graceful inclination
of her head, addressing a few polite words to one here and
there or extending her hand to be kissed by some distinguished stranger presented to her. Thus she made her way
to the gaming tables; once arrived there she became quite
human again and joked or laughed at some witty word or

repartee. At the stroke of ten, however, she invariably retired. The favourite bowed, gave her his arm and conducted her to her room—from which he did not emerge again that night. Thus her whole court, her son, her grandchildren became witnesses of her intimate life. In such moments she was no longer an empress, a mother, a grandmother, but only a woman.

Her grandchildren loved and revered her. She felt great affection and concern for them, whereas Paul, her son, had reason to complain of his mother's neglect. She even suffered her favourites to treat him with extreme insolence; but all her letters and actions testify to the place in her heart occupied by her grandchildren, particularly gentle Grand Duke Alexander. She took such detailed care of their education that their parents were deprived of every say in the matter. The girls were given the most honourable woman in Russia as their governess, while the boys were educated by tutors such as La Harpe. This appointment was certainly a noble gesture on the part of an autocratic ruler, for La Harpe, a free Swiss, was an out-and-out republican. He told her frankly that even as the tutor of princes he was unable to change his principles. Catherine replied: "Sir, you can be a Jacobin, a republican—anything you like; I consider you a man of honour, and that is enough for me." And this she said at the time when another crowned head, in France, was falling under the guillotine!

However loose and unrestrained her own conduct, she watched over her grandchildren's moral welfare with the greatest care. She observed their physical and mental development from early infancy and in her letters to her friends delighted in reporting the latest news of childish pranks, special characteristics and talents, and the health and well-being of the little Grand Dukes. If Alexander and Constantine later failed to fulfil all the hopes of their imperial grandmother, the fault was not hers: nature was stronger than upbringing. But Catherine's principles were sound. There is no denying that she strove to instil in her grandsons nobility and firmness of character, a clear judgment and purposeful energy. Alexander acquired some of those qualities, whereas Constantine's bad character resisted all improvement.

Catherine, though far from strict in her own morals, severely supervised those of her family circle. She never considered that her own mode of life constituted a bad example to her children and grandchildren. Everything she did seemed to her a matter of course, and she made no secret of her doings. Catherine's lack of morals had its root not so much in her character as in her time, and in the extraordinary circumstances that had brought her to the most powerful, but also to the most barbarous and corrupt of all courts.

CHAPTER XI

Catherine's End

THE LAST TEN YEARS of Catherine's reign showed her at the zenith of her renown and power. After the death of her great rival, Frederick the Great, her genius ruled Europe. She pulled the political strings at will. Crowned heads who quarrelled among themselves elected the Empress of Russia their arbiter and let her regulate the interests of their states. The whole world marvelled at her vast dominions, her inexhaustible resources, her brilliant court and the barbarian splendour of her courtiers, and admired her persistent good luck in all the enterprises dictated by her insatiable ambition on a giant scale.

Yet inside Russia everything was not so well as it seemed to the outside world. Russia was rotten at the core. Protected by the favourite, a handful of grandees shared out the empire among themselves, plundering state funds and revenues and oppressing the poor Russian people. Catherine was no longer the young, vigorous ruler of her early years but an old woman enthralled by her passion for a young man whom she idolised. She had put the welfare of her country into his hands. This youthful, arbitrary ruler was Plato Zubov.

At the age of sixty, Catherine's ever youthful heart spoke once again. This woman, so credulous in love, basked in the illusion of a new springtime of love. Twenty-two year-old Zubov was an even better actor than his predecessors. He employed sentimentality to find the way to Catherine's heart.

He was a dashing young lieutenant in the Horse Guards. That influential man, Field-Marshal Nikolai Saltikov, was his uncle and patron, and Zubov knew how to exploit the relationship. He was of very pleasing appearance, not particularly tall but lithe, slender and well-built. His features were aristocratic, while his dark eyes held a promise of tenderness and passion. His hair was beautiful: it shone like silk. Moreover, the young man was amiable, well bred and fairly well-read. He spoke several languages with fluency and had an ear for music—in short, he had all the qualities to seduce a young girl as well as an old woman. He took the greatest pains to display his accomplishments to best advantage in order to attract the Empress's notice. What else was needed but youth, beauty and boldness in order to win Catherine's favour? Beauty he had in ample measure, nor did he lack enterprise; but in addition he was extremely ambitious. The boldest plans took shape in his young head; but in order to realise them he must secure influential friends in the Empress's immediate entourage. His relationship to Saltikov was a great help. As a Guardsman he was also frequently on duty in Her Majesty's antechambers where Catherine's confidantes, Mesdames Protasov, Anne Narishkin and Pyerekustchina, more than once witnessed his ardent enthusiasm for his august Empress. In front of them he praised the Empress so assiduously that Catherine soon came to know of the young officer's deep attachment. Her ladies did not leave her in doubt that Plato Zubov was not merely full of admiration for his sovereign, but that the woman—at sixty!—had made a deep impression on his heart. Her vanity could not resist such a conquest.

In July, 1789 Zubov asked Nikolai Saltikov for a favour:

to appoint him commandant of the guardsmen attached to
Catherine's establishment in Czarskoe-Selo. Saltikov found
this convenient: he had long since noticed that Her Majesty
might be inclined to appoint a successor to Mamonov who
had recently fallen from favour. Plato Zubov seemed made
for the post, and he intended to use the young officer as
his tool against Potiomkin, whom he hated. Zubov's wish
was granted more quickly than he had dared to hope. On
the evening of his new appointment the Empress invited
him to supper. Catherine was taken with him, especially
as he was the only young and handsome officer near her at
the moment. Moreover, she was "on the rebound" from
Mamonov's rejection of her favours. On the following day
young Zubov was ordered to report to the Empress's
physician-in-ordinary and to Madame Protasov, her lady-in-
waiting. What these two reported must have been satisfactory to Her Majesty, for Zubov was appointed Adjutant-
General and moved into the apartments of the favourite
"en titre". That evening he led the Empress into the reception hall and at dinner sat at her right hand. Dignitaries
and courtiers stood cap-in-hand before the new star that
was rising. When Catherine left the gaming table she was
particularly cheerful and gay. Her face beamed with joy
and pride at having captured such a handsome youth. He
followed her into her bedroom, alone ... and court gossips
had fresh subject matter for interesting conjectures. Various comments were made on this latest whim of the Empress's.

"He is a well-mannered boy but of moderate intelligence;
I don't think he is going to hold his post for long. Besides,
I don't care", wrote Bezhborodko to Count Voronzov, Grand
Chancellor of the Realm and Princess Dashkov's uncle.

"An attractive young man, dark, slim, not very tall and
resembling a handsome Frenchman such as the Chevalier

ZUBOV

de Puységu", thought the Swedish Ambassador, Stedingk.

Catherine herself found young Zubov enchanting. Once again she came alive in the arms of this lover who did not seem to mind that she was almost obese. Her legs, continually swollen, had become shapeless lumps of flesh. Her face still bore traces of former beauty but—she was sixty. Her mouth was toothless, her chin sagged, her neck was wrinkled; only her white hands were still beautiful. Yet her heart still seemed to beat with the same youthful ardour as at the age of twenty-six when she had first received bold Saltikov in her room. "I have come to life again like a fly numbed by the cold", she wrote to far-away Potiomkin, "I am once again gay and in good health ... His (Zubov's) amiable character makes me amiable, too." She referred to him as "the child", "little blackie", "that lovely boy", and never failed to mention him in her letters to her friends.

But the "lovely boy" soon proved himself an ambitious, domineering and insatiable tyrant. He grabbed influence, offices and honours and filled his own pockets and those of his family with Catherine's gold. His amiability extended only to the Empress whom he knew how to flatter; the rest of humanity he treated like an inferior species. At the same time he was an utter ignoramus in public affairs and never troubled to learn. His policy, his conduct of affairs and his sybaritic luxury had a pernicious effect on the state: Russia's monument to the last favourite of Catherine the Great was an empty exchequer. His bad influence became more noticeable after the death of his rival, Potiomkin, who had at least commanded respect. In the seven years of his "reign" Zubov obtained all those dignities and honours which twenty years of real merit had procured for Potiomkin. Zubov was made a Prince, "Governor-General of New Russia", Inspector-General of Artillery, and received all the Russian and foreign decorations held by his predecessor, even the Orders of the Black and of the Red Eagle. In 1795 Count Rostopchin wrote to Simeon Voronzov: "Count Zubov is everything here. There is no will beside his. His power is greater than Prince Potiomkin's used to be. He is as negligent and incapable as ever, even though the Empress repeats on every occasion that he is the greatest genius ever produced by Russia."

Catherine did not or would not see that this favourite, through whose delicate hands the millions were running, was disrupting her state. Love and passion made her completely blind to the faults of this young coxcomb. When her first intoxication was over she also took his younger brother, Valerian, into her personal service. Both these licentious wastrels did their best to waste their imperial mistress's substance. Valerian, a short time after obtaining her highest favours, staked thirty thousand roubles on the turn of one card at faro—he who, a few weeks before, had been a penniless subaltern. Both Plato and Valerian dipped into public funds without having to give accounts. They and their partisans were always ready to sell jobs, titles, dignities, decorations, pardons, and even alliances and peace or war. The favourite's favourites wasted almost as much as Zubov himself. He was, however, much more subtle than his predecessors. He never asked Catherine for money and riches but extracted them by virtue of his unlimited power. He imposed excessive taxes on large estates, ruining their owners. Their estates became debt-ridden and finally passed to the state, that is, into Zubov's hands: he bought those lands with Catherine's money.

In Potiomkin's lifetime Catherine wanted to present her young lover with a palace Potiomkin wished to sell. One day at dinner she asked him in front of a numerous company how much he wanted for it. Potiomkin guessed her intention but did not wish this palace to pass into his rival's hands. He therefore replied calmly, though with some inner malignity: "Your Majesty will forgive me, but the castle is already sold."—"Since when?", asked the astonished Empress.—"Since this morning."—"To whom?"—"This is the buyer", and he pointed to a young adjudant of his, a penniless young officer who a minute ago had had no idea that he was going to be the owner of a large estate with 12,000 peasants. However, the trick had done its work and the Empress could do nothing. She soon made it up to her darling by giving him other presents, while singing the praise of his many virtues. She once wrote to him: "Never has one of your age held such powers nor possessed such gifts to serve his country."

The whole court knew of Catherine's blind spot for Zubov and in order to please her fawned upon the favourite in a disgusting manner. Aged generals, ministers who had grown grey in Her Majesty's service thronged the young fellow's ante-rooms and kow-towed as to an idol before this genius whom their sovereign's foresight had discovered. Inside, however, they cursed, hated and despised him for his arrogance. Once, he was pleased with his retinue to hunt a hare on the road from Petersburg to Czarskoe-Selo. For a full hour Zubov blocked the road with his carriages, attendants and hounds, not caring that he was holding up all traffic on this important route; courtiers in their carriages on their way to the Empress, couriers with dispatches, peasants who had to go to market were all made to miss their appointments: no one dared to proceed and interfere with the pleasures of almighty Zubov.

His levee resembled that of one of Louis XV's courtesans. From eight in the morning onward his ante-room was filled with ministers, courtiers, generals, foreign diplomats and other "V.I.P.'s" and petitioners of all kinds. Most of them would wait for four or five hours without being admitted.

The next day they waited again. If finally the great day came when His Grace deigned to give them an audience he would receive them in his dressing room, several at the time. He usually turned his back on those who entered, for he sat in front of a large mirror facing the door, having his silky locks curled and powdered. He did not once look at the crowd of courtiers who assembled in awed silence. He pretended being a very busy man and had his secretary read out the latest dispatches and letters. All the while his valet was powdering his hair, raising clouds of dust from which those present dared not recoil. If the conceited young man was not busy listening to his letters he gazed boredly at the ceiling, taking no notice of his callers. He seemed to concentrate entirely on the antics of his pet monkey who jumped from chandelier to curtain or on the heads of elderly courtiers. Some of them obediently inclined their heads to provide a landing ground for the favourite's little favourite. Somes are even said to have put more powder on their hair and to have put on higher wigs because the brute was known to have a preference for high toupets and plenty of powder. In this humiliating manner was the Empress's lover fawned upon. A high-ranking general and former ambassador to Constantinople, relates Rostopchin in one of his letters, insisted on personally preparing and serving a cup of Turkish coffee for the spoilt "child" every morning; others would come and kiss his hands while he was still in bed.

As long as his morning audience lasted no one dared to speak to Zubov. Should he condescend to distinguish a man by addressing him, the one so honoured would cautiously approach on tiptoe to receive a word from the Presence, and then tiptoe back to his place. General Langeron, a contemporary, relates that some people waited in Zubov's antechamber for three years without being spoken to by him, yet came again and again, lest they might incur his displeasure.

Catherine did not see all this. She was happier than ever. Young Zubov had insinuated himself into her heart. She fancied that she was educating him to be a support and image of her genius. Her love for him—as once for Lanskoy—was tinged with maternal feelings, only much more so. Zubov was her idol, her son, her child who "cried if not admitted to her room." This child made ageing Catherine young again. She gave entertainments and banquets and was gay as never before. She enjoyed seven years of untroubled happiness. Her sixty-seven years were hardly noticeable. Never did the small parties in the Hermitage forgather as often as in Catherine's last years; never was there as much laughter as in Zubov's time. Catherine's immense zest and vitality did not forsake her in her old age, and she tried her best to hide the inevitable symptoms of growing elderly. She would never appear tired and despite her great stoutness walked with short, quick steps. She hated old age and disliked being congratulated on her birthday, when another year was added to her age. Nor did she make a secret of this dislike. "I hate this day like the plague", she wrote, "a fine present, this, to add another year to my age; how I would like to miss it." And on August 18, 1796, only a few months before her death, she remarked in a letter to Grim: "Look well after yourself; as for me, I feel as light as a bird."

However, this birdlike lightness was far from being a fact. Catherine's legs kept swelling; she suffered from varicose veins that were aggravated by the slightest exertion, so that she could no longer climb stairs. The noblemen whose houses Catherine visited on gala occasions replaced their staircases with gently sloping ramps to save her climbing stairs. A Prince once had to spend a small fortune on having all stairs in his house remodelled and carpeted with precious rugs. Catherine usually had to use a stick when walking: her feet alone would no longer support her heavy body. She disliked this, as she hated everything that reminded her of her age. With her beautiful favourite whom she loved almost to distraction, she forgot everything: old age, shapeless figure, faded charms; she obeyed only the dictates of her passionate heart. She imagined that Zubov loved her, though he was merely pretending a sentiment he did not feel. Ambition alone made him play the part he acted so well.

As a monarch, Catherine now stood at the summit of her power and greatness—the result of her astute policies and tireless labours. Yet in her heart of hearts she had to suffer many disappointments, though she would not admit it, because she wanted to be deceived. How could a woman of such genius and intelligence have failed to notice that in her later years she lacked capable generals, faithful and conscientious stewards? That the growing luxury and tremendous wastefulness of Zubov and his creatures—not forgetting her own—were unbalancing the state's budget? That ruined finances and a disrupted administration, combined with the poverty of the people, were in sharp contrast to the brilliancy of her court? Catherine knew moments of tiredness. Success of all her undertakings was indispensable to her; any failure hit her so much the harder. She would occasionally complain to those near her, but never did a word of worry or reproach to Zubov come over her lips. She hid her sorrows from him: she must be gay and merry to please him.

The hardest blow ever to fall on this woman so used to political success was young King Gustavus Adolphus IV of Sweden's refusal to sign his marriage contract with her granddaughter, Grand Duchess Alexandrine, in the fall of

1796. It was Catherine's dearest wish to effect this union, which would have brought her great political advantage. Having used her powerful influence to frustrate another marriage projected by the young king—to a princess of Mecklenburg—she invited the young man to Petersburg together with his Regent, Duke Charles of Södermanland. Gustavus made the best impression at court. He was a slender, handsome youth of refined manners that contrasted strongly with the uncouth behaviour of Grand Duke Constantine. During this visit Catherine was all life and cheerfulness; she gave brilliant parties and balls and was herself among the gayest of all. She was about to see her dearest wish come true. Delightful fifteen-year old Alexandrine and the young king seemed to cherish a real affection for each other; there was mutual interest, to put it at its lowest. When Catherine thought the time ripe for their betrothal she appointed a day on which she assembled the entire court, the Senate and the clergy. They were to witness the great Empress awarding a royal throne to her granddaughter. That night Catherine shone in splendour, wearing the imperial purple cloak and her crown as she sat beneath the canopy of her throne. With great excitement everyone was looking forward to the arrival of the young king into whose hand she was to place the Grand Duchess's

But proud Catherine and her court waited for the groom in vain. He did not come. Catherine had omitted to make arrangements concerning the bride's religious faith. The king had assumed that Alexandrine was going to embrace Protestantism; but when he read in the draft contract submitted to him by Zubov and Markov that the Grand Duchess must have a Greek chapel and an Orthodox priest in her husband's palace, Gustavus refused to sign. He remained deaf to all entreaties, even when Swedish diplomatists intervened. The Empress and her court had to withdraw without having seen him. Never had Catherine suffered such humiliation, and at the hands of a seventeen year old prince. Yet only for a brief moment did she allow her shock at this insult to overcome her. When the favourite came and whispered this news into her ear she sat for a few instants, staring speechlessly into space; than she dismissed her court and on Zubov's arm retired to her rooms. Here she is said to have shown symptoms of a slight apoplectic stroke. At any rate she passed an extremely unpleasant and painful night. She herself remarked next morning that she had found the night before her accession less restless than this one. We remember that on the night of June 27/28, 1762, Catherine slept so soundly that Alexei Orlov had to rouse her at five in the morning in order to acquaint her with the position.

King Gustavus did not, however, quit the Russian capital immediately after this scene. Negotiations were still pending, and Catherine even gave a ball at which she and the young king appeared and Alexandrine was also present. But Gustavus remained inexorable. Throughout the evening he did not address a single word to Alexandrine but danced with other princesses. The rupture was manifest. The Empress had suffered the hardest blow of her life—failure. She had been over-confident in placing her affairs into Zubov's and Markov's inexperienced hands. Her pride did not suffer her to evince the slightest sign of regret at this defeat, but the hurt bit deeply into her soul. Her health deteriorated rapidly. She had always derided superstition, but when she saw a shooting star in Augst, 1796 she said that this signified her early death.

It was another sign of old age that this otherwise clearsighted woman placed herself in the hands of a notorious quack and adventurer, Lambro-Cazzioni. He claimed that he could heal her swollen legs by means of daily foot-baths in ice-cold sea water. In order to make his treatment more impressive he fetched the water from the sea himself. At first the treatment did her good, and she joked with Lambro at the expense of orthodox practitioners and their methods. But soon congestion of the blood vessels and colics made their appearance, forcing her to give up the baths. Her condition changed from day to day, now for the better, now for the worse. On some days she moved with the greatest difficulty, leaning heavily on Zubov's arm and supported on the other side by a footman or a maid. On other days again she would feel quite comfortable. November 5, 1796, was a particularly good day. At that day's session in the Hermitage Catherine laughed more than ever. Leon Narishkin had dressed up as a pedlar and haggled with the Empress over the various toys and knick-knacks he drew from his inexhaustible pockets. Catherine was very fond of such pleasantries. That night she was in very good spirits, having just had the good news that General Moreau had been forced to retreat across the Rhine. She immediately drafted a jocular letter to the Austrian Ambassador, Cobenzl, wherein she said: *"Je m'empresses d'annoncer à l'excellente Excellence que les excellentes troupes de l'excellente cour ont complètement battu les Français."* All at once, however, she retired on Zubov's arm, earlier than customary, with the characteristic remark that she had the stomach-ache from having laughed so much.

Next morning Catherine rose as usual at six. She sent for Zubov, worked with her secretaries and dealt with various matters. Than she desired to be left alone for some moments, till she would call her private secretary. He was waiting in an anteroom. Some considerable time passed, but nothing was heard of the Empress. People became worried and listened at the door: nothing moved in Catherine's rooms. Neither the secretary nor others of her retinue

dared to enter her room contrary to orders: she had wanted
to be alone. After waiting a little longer her valet Zotov
finally brought himself to open her bedroom door. The
Empress was not there, nor was she in her dressing room.
Zotov walked on—suddenly he uttered a piercing scream:
in a passage leading to her privy the Empress lay on the
ground, unconscious, with foam at her mouth.

Legend has invented a shameful story about the place
where Catherine suffered her fatal stroke. It is alleged that
she had Poniatovsky velvet-upholstered throne put there
for a purpose that need not be described. Catherine, however, cannot be considered capable of so low and ignoble
an action.

The unconscious Empress was carried back to her bedroom. As she was very heavy her servants were unable to
lift her on the bed and placed her on a mattress on the
floor. There was universal consternation. The doctors declared that there was no hope: Catherine had had a para-
lytic stroke. Her agony was to last another thirty-seven
hours, but she did not recover her speech. Some thought
this a lucky circumstance for Paul whom she would otherwise have excluded from the succession.

In Catherine the world lost a gifted personality, a darling of the Fates, a genius with all the qualities and defects
implied in the word. Her passing left her inner circle in the
greatest consternation. Admiral Shishkov describes in his
memoirs the panic caused in the Winter Palace by Catherine's death. He had arrived on November 6 in order to
attend Zubov's customary levee, and had no inkling of what
had happened. As he entered the reception room he was
greatly astonished to find it quite empty. Only the quack,
Lambro-Cazzioni, stood there, pale as death, staring fixedly
with wide-open eyes at the Admiral as he came in. He made
no movement and did not reply to the Admiral's questions.

Then Zubov's brother Nikolai came in, he, too, thunder-struck and speechless. Shishkov withdrew. On the stairs he encountered the Empress's secretary and asked him what had happened. The young man's entire body trembled, but he did not manage to utter a single word. Now a nervous tremor seized the Admiral as well. He rushed home without having learned the news and took to his bed with a high fever. Something terrible must have happened in the Palace: he sensed that it could only be the Empress's death.

Zubov was most affected by the event. Catherine's death hurled him back into nothingness, for he could expect nothing good of Paul. Not only had Zubov been treating the Grand Duke with the utmost contempt and arrogance, but Paul on general principles disliked his mother and her entourage. It sufficed to have been on good terms with his mother to have him for one's enemy for ever. Zubov saw everything collapse into ruin. He wept scalding tears for the loss, not of his beloved but of his benefactress, his potent patroness, the source of his fame and fortune. For ten days he locked himself in the house of his sister, Countess Yerebzov, refusing to go out or see anyone. He dreaded his fate which now lay in the new Czar's hands. He had never shown attachment or respect for Paul and now feared his revenge. The flatterers had abandoned the once powerful favourite. He was hated, discarded, a back number. The Empress's body was still lying in state when all eyes turned towards the new Czar and everyone endeavoured to get into his good graces. To win the favour of this new court which was feared rather than loved was everybody's aim.

At last a courier from Paul I came to Zubov. He told him that the Czar had furnished a house for him and, to-gether with the Czarina, was coming there the next day to take a dish of tea. Zubov did not believe his ears, but it was true. Paul had put at his disposal a handsomely appointed house in Morskaya Street, complete with stables, staff etc. And on the morrow Paul, together with his Empress, did indeed visit the former lover of his mother in his new home. Zubov prostrated himself, but Paul kindly bade him rise and quoted an ancient Russian proverb to the effect that "he who remembers past offence deserves to lose an eye." Such language from Paul, who was known as morose and misanthropic, increased Zubov's amazement. A footman was serving champagne. The Emperor took a glass, half-emptied it and said: "I wish you as many years of happiness as there are drops left in this glass." Zubov thanked him, though feeling some misgivings. Thereupon Paul invited his consort to pour out the tea for his mother's favourite. "You know", he added with biting sarcasm, "there is no 'mistress' in this house." Zubov bit his lip.

This little scene took place on November 29, 1796. Only two months later, on January 17, 1796, Zubov knew that his part at the Czar's court was over for good. Paul, who had at first treated him so kindly, dismissed him from all his offices and dignities and in addition sequestrated all his estates. An imperial ukase gave Catherine's former favourite permission to travel abroad—in other words, banished him from Russia. Now Zubov hated Catherine's son more than ever. He went to Germany and spent some time in the resort of Teplitz which had recently become fashionable. There, his numerous amours, especially his relations with charming Countess La Roche-Aymond, and of course his having been the last lover of the great Empress, provided the latest scandal for visitors. A short time afterwards he fell in love with one of the young duchesses of Courland, said to be the richest heiresses in Europe. The old Duke, however, whom Zubov had deprived of his principality, had sufficient pride not to marry his daughter to the ex-

PAUL I

favourite of the Russian Empress. Zubov would have been capable of eloping with the young princess, but suddenly he received a message from Paul—probably at the instigation of Pahlen—ordering him back to the court of Petersburg. Paul did not realise that he was bringing back his mortal enemy. In 1801 Zubov took part in the assassination of the unfortunate Czar. In murdering the son of his mistress he avenged the disgrace he had suffered.

Alexander I treated him with cold indifference, like all the partners in that plot, and intimated that he would rather have him away from court. Zubov was too vain to play the part of outcast, and once again travelled in Germany. Later he lived in his castle at Shavle in Poland which Paul I, after impounding it, had released. Zubov, the former spendthrift, became a great miser in middle age, thinking only of increasing his wealth and concealing bags of money in his cellars.

At the age of fifty love once again knocked on his door. This time his choice fell on no empress nor princess or even a countess, but a simple young girl, Thekla Valentinovitch, the daughter of a small property owner. He saw her in the street one day and immediately sent his steward to bring her to the castle as his mistress. But for the first time in his life he encountered resistance. Both the parents and the girl stubbornly resisted his advances, despite all the great man's golden promises: it was marriage or nothing. Zubov was in love and consented; but he enjoyed his new-found happiness for only another year. Then he died, and young Princess Zubov inherited the twenty million roubles which Catherine's generous hand had given to her favourite.

APPENDIX I

CATHERINE IN HER LETTERS
(by Thomas Fassam)

Catherine was an avid personality—avid for everything that life had to offer; and her appetite extended
widely in the realm of ideas. In her voluminous correspondence, which touched most of the famous intellects
of her life-time, she captured heads with the facility
that she enslaved hearts. The savants and men of letters
and fashion with whom she corresponded became not
only her intellectual devotees, but busied themselves
about Europe with commissions large and small; the
purchase of objects d'art, of books, of furnishings and
the distribution to deserving artist and writers of the
generous gifts dictated by her keen sense of herself as
a patron of whatever was new or noble.

One of her longest and most fascinating correspon-
dences was with Voltaire, with whom she discussed her
"Grand Instructions for the Code of Russia", an ambitious attempt to draw up a legal system based on the
dawning libertarian ideas that have become axioms to
lawgivers to-day.

The correspondence begins trivially enough. Voltaire
had rendered her a small service, and after a few pre-
liminary skirmishes on courtly levels, the two are plunged deeply in political disscussion.

September 30, 1765. Voltaire to Catherine:

I have yet another happiness: which is that all·those who have been honoured by Your Majesty's kindnesses are my friends; I hold myself indebted to you for what you have so generously done for the Diderots, the d'Alemberts, the Calas. All the men of letters in Europe should be at your feet...

Dare I say, Madame, that I am a little sorry you should be named Catherine? The heroines of bygone days never took the names of saints; Homer or Virgil would have been greatly embarassed by such names; and you were not made for the Calendar. But be you Juno, Minerva, Venus or Ceres (names which assimilate better into the poetry of all nations) I place myself at your Imperial Majesty's feet, with gratitude and the deepest respect .

November 17/28, 1765: Catherine to Voltaire

My head is as hard as my name is unharmonious... As I do not consider I have the right to be sung by poets, I shall not change my name for that of the envious and jealous Juno; I have not enough presumption to take that of Minerva; and I do not want the name of Venus—that fine lady has too much to answer for. Neither am I Ceres: the harvest in Russia this year has been a bad one: my own name at any rate leads me to hope for the intercession of my patron saint, wherever she may be, and taking it all in all I think it is the best name for me...

29 June/20 July, 1766: Catherine to Voltaire:

I read with great attention the printed matter which came with your letter. It is difficult to reduce to practice the principles it contains. Unfortunately the majority will oppose it for some time yet. But nevertheless it is possible to take the sting out of opinions which lead to the destruction of human lives.

Here, word for word, is what I have inserted among other matters in an instruction on this subject to the committee which will recast our laws:

'In a great empire, which extends its domination over as many diverse peoples as there are different faiths among men, the sin most damaging to the peace and tranquillity of its citizens would be intolerance of their respective religions. Nothing but a wise toleration, applied as much to orthodox religion as to politics, can bring the wandering sheep back to the true faith. Persecution exacerbates the spirit; tolerance sweetens it and renders it less obstinate; it snuffs out those disputes that are contrary to the calm of the state and the unity of its people.'

This kind of opinion, coming from an absolute ruler, was such as to gratify Voltaire. He became an unwavering partisan of Russia, and followed the fortunes of her military attempt to wrest Constantinople from the Turks with an anxiety that is the theme of many of his letters. But he never allowed Catherine to overlook the "Grand Instruction", and when it seemed the war was over wrote her again on the matter:

October 30, 1769: Voltaire to Catherine:

So here is my legislatrix entirely victorious! I do not know whether they have tried in Paris or Constantinople to suppress your 'Instructions for the Code of Russia'; but I know that they should conceal it from the French; it is a too shameful reproach to us on our antiquated, ridiculous and barbarous legal system, which is almost entirely founded on the decretals of Popes and on ecclesiastical jurisprudence.

March 5/16, 1771: Catherine to Voltaire:

Certainly, Monsieur, in the war which the Sultan un-
justly declared on me, a good deal of what you say will
be done; but for the present one cannot succeed in doing
anything but making proposals on the different branches
of the great tree of legislation according to my principles,
which have been printed and which you know. We are very
busy fighting; and this distracts us too much from giving
proper concentration to this great work.

> Voltaire knew, certainly, that the Empress's legal
> theories had been printed. They were proscribed in
> Paris as a seditious document!

July 10th, 1771: Voltaire to Catherine:

Here are the facts: a library in Holland prints the "Instructions", which should be the manual of every king and
every tribunal in the world. It sends to Paris a bale of two
thousand copies. The book is passed for examination to a
bumpkin book censor as though it were some ordinary work
—as though any Paris blackguard could be judge of the
ordinances of a sovereign—and what a sovereign! This
clod-hopping dolt finds it includes propositions that are
daring, scandalous offensive to a Welch ear (Ed. Note:
Voltaire's name for the French when they annoyed him
was 'les Welches'—as we might say 'The Vandals' or 'Phi-
listines'); he reports it to the Chancellery as a dangerous
book and they send it back to Holland without further
examination.

'A government must be such that one citizen cannot fear
another, but all fear the laws.'

'Nothing should be forbidden by law that is not hurtful
to the individual in particular or to society in general.'

— Are these the maxims that the Welch do not wish

to accept? They deserve .. they deserve .. they deserve ..
all that they get.

September 15/15, 1771: Catherine to Voltaire:

I haven't the slightest liking for the events in your
country which you report to me. If the beautiful arms of
the beautiful dancers of the Paris Opera or Opéra Comique
(which are the wonder of the world) console France for
the destruction of her parliaments and for her new taxes,
after eight years of peace, one must admit that they are
essential services that have been rendered to the government. But when these taxes have been imposed, will the
King's coffers be filled, and the state liberated?

Catherine expressed herself quite freely in her letters
on the subject of French politics. As we see in the
letters of Grimm, her correspondents sometimes suffered for this! Her exhanges with Voltaire were not, however, entirely political; she deferred to him as a writer,
and when she was trying to stimulate interest in the
drama among her people often conssulted him on practical questions.

Jan 30/Feb. 10, 1772: Catherine to Voltaire:

In one of your letters you wish me, among other fine
things that your friendship for me inspires, a greater access of pleasures: I am going to discus with you a kind
of pleasure that is very absorbing to me, and on which
I pray you to give me your advice.

You know—since nothing escapes you—that five hundred young ladies are being trained in a house formerly
devoted to three hundred brides of Our Lord. These young
women, I must admit, exceed our hopes for them: they
make astonishing progress and everyone agrees that they
are becoming as agreeable as they are filled with knowledge

useful to society. They are of irreproachable behaviour, without at the same time sharing the fastidious austerity of recluses. For the past two winters we have been making them perform tragedies and comedies, and they acquit themselves beter than those who act professionally here; but I confess that there are few works which suit them, since their preceptors wish to avoid encouraging them to play parts which will stir the passions too early in life. There is too much love, it is said, in French plays, and even the best authors have been influenced by this national taste or characteristic. To have plays specially written is impossible; they are not bespoke works, but the fruits of genius. Poor or insipid plays would spoil our tastes. What ought we to do? then I know nothing about it, and so appeal to you. Ought we to choose only scenes? but that is far less interesting, in my view, than complete plays.

March 12th, 1772: Voltaire to Catherine:

It is true that all our plays are about love: it is a passion for which I have the greatest respect; but I think, like Your Majesty, that it should not develop very early in life. One could, I think, remove from certain selected comedies the passages most dangerous to young hearts, leaving the interest of the play intact; there would probably not be twenty lines to change in "Le Misanthrope' and not forty in 'L'Avare'... I will have some unbound tragedies and comedies sent from Paris and have them bound up with blank pages on which I will write such changes as are necessary to protect the virtue of your beautiful young ladies...

Here in a letter during the same month, is a glimpse of what kind of scandal was already surrounding the name of the Empress: "I know the ballad-mongers of Paris have spread it abroad that I have taken on my eighth man: it is a coarse lie, and devoid of common sense. Apparently there are people among you who like to be misled; they must be left to that pleasure, for everything is for the best in this best of all possible worlds, according to Dr. Pangloss."

She took this kind of irritation from whence it came. Her view was that her private life was her own affair; and that it was more important to press forward with her activities as a liberalising and modernising monarch.

Sept. 20/Oct. 1, 1777: Catherine to Voltaire:

Our legislative edifice rears itself little by little: the 'Instruction for the Code' is its foundation: I sent it to you ten years ago. You will see that the laws do not depart from those principles, but spring from them; soon they will be followed by those concerning finance, commerce, the police, etc, on which we have been busy for the past two years: after which the code will be nothing but an easy and simple work to draw up.

This is my idea of the criminal code. Crimes cannot be great in number; but to fit the punishment to the crime necessitates, I think, a separate enterprise and a great deal of reflection. I think that the nature and weight of evidence could be reduced to a very methodical and simple form of questioning which would elucidate the facts. I am persuaded, and have established, that the best and surest criminal procedure is one which passes this kind of case through three courts within a stated time; without which the personal security of the accused would be at the mercy of the passions, of ignorance, of unintentional mistake or hot-headedness.

These precautions might not please the so-called Holy Office; but reason has its rights, against which sooner or later stupidity and prejudice will batter themselves to pieces.

Shortly before his death Voltaire received a copy of the new Russian laws in German and started the enterprise of having them translated into "Welch". "It will be read in Chinese, in all languages" he wrote to Catherine. "It will become the evangel of the universe. I was right when I said, thirteen years ago, that everything would come to us from the North Star."

What was it that came from the "North Star"? A synthesis of liberal thought of the time, which Catherine never pretended was her own original and unaided work. What was significant about the "Grand Instructions" was that they emanated from an Empress who was the most absolute of absolute monarchs; and it was not without significance, either, that they fairly successfully preserved the authorithy of the monarch without the overt expression of reactionary ideas. Catherine, at any rate, did not think that the repressions that prevailed in France were the only way to keep a king on his throne; and however much she may have deplored the events of 1789 and the years of terror which followed, she appreciated that they were as much due to harsh government as to the natural blacguardism of the revolutionary leaders as it appeared to her.

The "Grand Instructions" are worth stsudying in detail. Here are liberal quotations from the original Englishtranslation, in which there are propositions that would hardly disgrace Russia to-day.

1.   The Christian law teaches us to do mutual good to one another, as much as we possibly can.

2. Laying this down as a fundamental Rule prescribed by religion, which has taken or ought to take Root in the Hearts of the whole People! we cannot but suppose that every honest man in the Realm is, or will be, desirous of seeing his native Country at the very Summit of Happiness, Glory, Safety and Tranquillity.

3. And that every Individual Citizen in particular must wish to see himself protected by Laws, which should not distress him in his circumstances but, on the contrary, should defend him from all Attempts of others that are repugnant to this fundamental Rule.

4. In order therefore to proceed to a speedy Execution of what We expect from such a general Wish WE, fixing the Foundation upon the first-mentioned Rule, ought to begin with an Inquiry into the Natural situation of this Empire.

5. For those Laws have the greatest Conformity with Nature, whose particular Regulations are best adapted to the Situation and Circumstances of the People for whom they are instituted.

6. Russia is an European State.

8. The Possessions of the Russian Empire extend upon the terrestrial globe to 32 degrees of Latitude and to 165 of Longitude.

9. The Sovereign is absolute; for there is no other Authority but that which centres in his single Person, that can act with a Vigour proportionate to the extent of such a vast Dominion.

13. What is the true End of Monarchy? Not to deprive People of their natural Liberty; but to correct their Actions in order to attain the *supreme good*.

15. The Intention and the End of Monarchy is the Glory of the Citizen, of the State, and of the Sovereign.

20. The Laws, which form the Foundation of the State,

send out certain Courts of Judicature through which, as through smaller Streams, the power of the Government is poured out and diffused.

21.   The Laws allow these Courts of Judicature to remonstrate that such or such an Injunction is unconstitutional, and prejudicial, obscure and impossible to be carried into Execution; and direct beforehand to which injunction one ought to pay Obedience, and in what Manner one ought to conform to it. These laws undoubtedly constitute the firm and immovable basis of every State.

22.   There must be a political Body, to whom the Care and strict Execution of these Laws ought to be confided.

32.   It is the greatest Happiness for a man to be so circumstanced that if his Passions should prompt him to be mischievous, he should still think it more for his Interest not to give Way to them.

34.   The equality of citizens consists in this: that they should all be subject to the same laws.

35.   This Equality requires Institutions so well adapted as to prevent the Rich from oppressing those who are not so wealthy as themselves, and converting all the Charges and Employments entrusted to them as Magistrates only to their own private Emolument.

366.   General or political Liberty does not consist in that licentious Notion, *that a Man may do whatever he pleases.*

39.   The political Liberty of a Citizen is the Peace of Mind arising from a Consciousness that every Individual enjoys his peculiar Safety; and in order that the People might attain this Liberty, the laws ought to be so framed that no one Citizen should stand in Fear of another; but that all of them should stand in Fear of the same Laws.

41.   Nothing ought to be forbidden by the Laws but what may be prejudicial, either to every Individual in particular, or to the whole community in general.

43.   To preserve Laws from being violated, they ought to be so good, and so well furnished with all Expedients tending to produce the greatest possible Good to the People that every Individual might be fully convinced that it was his Interest as well as his Duty to preserve the Laws inviolable.

(Here follows a long dissertation on the laws and customs of other countries, expounding the theory that the laws which govern mankind are a conglomeration of the religion and climate of the country and the example set by past ages in manners and customs).

60.   If there should be a necessity of making great alterations amongst the People for their greater benefit, that must be corrected by Laws which has been instituted by Laws, and that must be amended by Custom which has been introduced by Custom; and it is extreme bad Policy to alter that by Law which ought to be altered by Custom. 67.   Civil Liberty flourishes when the Laws deduce every Punishment from the peculiar Nature of every Crime. The Application of Punishment ought not to proceed from the arbitrary will or mere caprice of the legislator, but from the Nature of the Crime; and it is not the Man who ought to do Violence to a Man, but the proper Action of the Man himself.
68.   Crimes are divisible into four classes.
69.   The first Class of Crimes is that against Religion.
70.   The second, against Manners.
71.   The third, against the Peace.
72.   The fourth, against the Security of the Citizens.
73.   The Punishments inflicted upon these ought to flow from the Specific Nature of the very Crime.
81.   The Love of our Country, Shame and the Dread of

Public Censure are Motives which restrain, and may deter, Mankind from the Commission of a Number of Crimes.

82.   The greatest Punishment for a bad Action under a mild Administration will be for the Party to be convicted of it. The civil Laws will there correct Vice with the more Ease, and will not be under a necessity of employing more rigorious means.

83.   In these Governments, the Legislature will apply itself more to prevent Crimes than to punish them, and should take more Care to instil Good Manners into the Minds of the Citizens than to dispirit them by the Terror of Corporal and Capital Punishments.

96.   Good laws keep strictly a just medium. They do not always inflict pecuniary loss, nor always subject Malefactors to Corporal Punishment. All punishments by which the Human Body might be maimed ought to be abolished.

98.   The Power of a Judge consists only in a due Execution of the Laws, to the end that no Doubt might arise with respect to the Liberty and Security of the Citizens.

With such general propositions the Empress directs her lawgivers. Then, with characteristic energy, she gets down to detail. The form of procedure she recommends is genial, and at times novel. Judges are to enter into the minutest and most subtle details of the cases before them, and must give the defendant every chance to hear and study all the evidence against him so that he may be able to defend himself or choose someone to speak for him. Catherine considers that a minimum of two witnesses ought to give evidence, and that torture ought not to be resorted to "except only in those Cases where the Prisoner at the Bar refuses to plead!" She also insists on the right of those to be tried for capital offences to choose their own judges or at least to reject any they do not like; and adds, echoing Magna Carta, that some of the judges should be of the same rank as the accused.

Judges in Catherine's system are not supposed to try and interpret the law: what is the need when they can refer to the code? They are to concern themselves with finding the guilt or otherwise of the accused. If a man is taken into custody he is to be confined only for as long as it takes to prepare the case against him—for as short a while and as "gently" as possible. The burden of proof rests on the courts.

The laws ought to be written in the common vernacular tongue, and published as cheaply as the catechism: so that in schools children can be taught to read alternatively out of Church and Law books.

"Proofs from fact demonstrate to us" she writes, "that the frequent use of capital punishment never mended the morals of a people ... In a reign of peace and tranquillity, under a government established with the united wishes of the whole people; in a state well fortified against external enemies and protected within by strong supports ... there can be *no* necessity for *taking away the life* of a citizen ..."

Having stated guardedly that the aquality of citizens consists in being all subject to the same laws, Catherine qualifies this with reservations obviously based on contemporary custom:

250. A Society of Citizens, as well as everything else, requires a certain fixed Order. There ought to be *some to govern*, and *others to obey*.   . . . .

— to which she adds: ". . . we are obliged to alleviate the Situation of the Subjects as much as sound Reason will permit. And therefore to shun all Occasions of re-

ducing People to a State of Slavery, except the *utmost*
necessity should *inevitably* oblige us to do it. However,
it is still highly necessary to prevent those Causes
which so frequently incited Slaves to rebel against their
masters; but till these Causess are discovered it is impossible to prevent the like accidents by laws; though
the tranquillity both of the one and of the other depends
upon it."

Catherine was much perturbed at the great deficien-
cy of population in her empire, particularly those parts
of it which extended over vast tracts of country with
an insufficient number of people to improve the land.
She realised, and stressed, that overwhelming taxes
would make the population desert the countries or provinces in which they were unfairly taxed; and urged
that the population would increase if more attention
were paid to the health of the people and the careful
and industrious enjoyed the means of supporting themselves and their families.

The land was, in fact, very much in her mind and
heart; as it must be for any ruler of Russia.

294.   There can be neither skilful Handicrafts nor a firmly-
established Commerce, where Agriculture is neglected or
carried on with supineness and negligence.

313.   Agriculture is the first and principal Labour, which
ought to be encouraged in the people. The next is the manu-
facturing of our own produce.

Her policy has at times a familiar ring. Subsidies
were included in it, though they were only given to
those who did better than their neighbours. The same
kind of inducement was to be given to craftsmen whose
work was of a better order. Craftsmen she wanted to
encourage: machines she was not so sure about, fearing

that if they saved labour they would necessitate a population smaller than that she hoped for. She was a protectionist. "What cramps the trader does not necessarily cramp trade" was her attitude, "and while tariffs might cramp the individual they would on the whole benefit the commerce of the Nation."

The paternal state was represented in her thesis, too:

346.   An Alms bestowed on a Beggar in the Street can never acquit a State of the Obligation it lies under, of affording all its Citizens a certain Support during Life; such as wholesome Food, proper Clothing, and a Way of Life not prejudicial to Health in general.

Such was the duty of the state, according to Catherine; and the individual had for his part a duty to the state. Parents, for example, were very specifically instructed in their responsibility for putting into effect the rules of education, which were "the fundamental instutes which train us up to be citizens." The first duty of the parent was to teach the child the fear of God, the love of coutry, and respect for the established laws. Further, every parent should refrain from setting his children a bad example, by violence, sneering, lying and so forth. Parents were "to encourage in the child every laudable Inclination, to give them a desire for work and a dislike of idleness, and to instil into them those qualities and virtues by which they may prove real Citizens, useful members of the Community, and Ornaments to their Country." Elsewhere, Catherine adds to this that "a father may enrich his son more by giving him a good trade than by leaving him an inheritance."

She did not, however, believe that inheritance, either of wealth or title, was a particularly bad thing. Society asshe saw it was composed of horizontal strata, and would remain so; and in the ordinances connected with the class character of society she defines rather than justifies it at any length:

358.   The Husbandman, who cultivate the Lands and produce Food for People in every Rank of Life, live in country Towns and Villages. *This is their lot.*

359.   The Burghers, who employ their time in Mechanick Trades, Commerce, Atrs and Sciences, *inhabit the cities.*

360.   *Nobility* is an appellation of *Honour*, which distinguishes all those who are adorned by it from every other person of *inferior rank.*

363.   *Virtue* with *Merit* raises people to the Rank of Nobility.

What of those who were neither peasants, cits or aristocrats? They were, in Catherine's scheme of things, "the Middling Sort of People." "People of this rank" she laid down, "will enjoy a State of Liberty, without intermixing either with the Nobility or the Husbandmen. To this rank of People we ought to annex all those who are neither Gentlemen or Husbandmen; but employ themselves in Arts, Sciences, Navigation, Commerce or handicraft Trades." People educated in schools and colleges and the children of people belonging to the law were included in this class, the whole qualification for membership of it being based on "good manners and industry" and exclusion from it on "Perfidousness and Breach of Promise, especially if caused by Idleness and Treachery."

As we have already seen, the fact that the Empress consigned the artist to "the middling sort of people" was rather due to his unclassifiable character than to any lack of respect. Her absorption in matters of cul-

ture was chronic, and among those who ministered to
it best and longest was Baron Grimm, her friend and
correspondent for twenty-two years. Grimm was the
ideal man to act as cultural agent for the Empress in
Europe. He was a recognised authority, author of a
periodical letter on artistic and other matters which
circulated by subscription among the great. He was
also capable of seeing Catherine as a woman: Voltaire
never quite destroyed the relation of monarch to pe-
titioner, and the Empress never wrote to him so in-
timately as she did to Grimm.

April 25, 1774: Catherine to Grimm:

...I congratulate you on the great pleasure you have
had in celebrating the forty-sixth anniversary of my birth
in Courland. I hate that day like the plague: what a lovely
present it has bestowed on me! Each time it confers on
me the gift of another year, a thing which I could very
well do without. Be frank—it would be a charming thing,
an Empress who was no older than fifteen all her life.

Letters like this are interpersed among a host dealing
with the purchase of beautiful things for Catherine's
palaces. She had verij definite tastes, often on the
austere side, and a great capacity for neatly-turned
criticism:

January 20th, 1776: Catherine to Grimm:

I promised to relate to you the first impression that I
received from Huber's pictures; but I hardly know how to
fulfil my promise having regard to the circumstances. On
my arrival at Tsarskoe Selo I found the pictures in a rather
dark and excessively cold place; so that I was not especially
struck, and only burst out laughing at the "Lever du Pa-

triarche"; this man, in my opinion, is an original—the liveliness of his nature and the impetuosity of his imagination do not give him a chance to do one thing at a time. The cavorting horse, with Voltaire reining it, is even better. The disorder of his gig delighted me ... But what must I do for this great Huber since he has yielded up his pictures to me? Do tell me, clearly and specifically.

One of the more amusing passages of this correspondence concerns a writing-desk which Grimm was having made for the Empress.She first ordered it in 1777, and its achievement was attended with such delays and distractions that she wrote to him: "every time you mention the escritoire I await some new mortification, and the words escritoire and jeremiad are becoming synonymous with me. I will willingly pay everything that must be paid, and you must distribute gifts, compliments, thanks to whomever you see fit in this matter of the famous escritoire—only so long as you are happy yourself and that I hear no more about it."

The "famous escritoire" cost in the end 36,000 livres, and when it was finished a new chapter of annoyances began. Grimm ha to go through incredible formalities to get it to Russia.

April 22nd, 1778: Grimm to Catherine:

Such documents, emanating from the Holy of Holies of the Paris police, will no doubt figure prominently in the archives of the Empire—to prove to the remotest posterity that if one had conceived, though out and executed in Paris a writing-desk worthy of none but Catherine II, it would never have been finished without the wretched Paris police having a finger in the pie by direct order of the Government.

Among the artists from whom Grimm commissioned work for Catherine was Houdon, and she was awaiting news of his famous bust of Voltaire when the bitter blow of the master's death at Ferney reached her.

June 21st, 1778: Catherine to Grimm:

Up till now I had hoped that the news of Voltaire's death had been false; but you confirmed it, and suddenly I felt an emotion of universal discouragement and of contempt for the things of this world. The month of May has been fatal for me: I have lost two men who loved me and whom I honoured: Voltaire and Milord Chatham (William Pitt—Ed.). Not for a long time (and probably never as far as the first-named is concerned) will they be replaced by equals, and never by superiors: and for me they are irrevocably lost. I want to weep.

Can it be, however, that people honour and dishonour, act fairly and unfairly, anywhere so loftily as where you are? They publicly honoured, only a few weeks ago, a man whom to-day they dare not bury—and what a man! The fiirst of his nation ... Why didn't you get posession of his body, in my name? You should have sent him to me—you have lacked common-sense for the first time in your life—and I promise you he would have had the richest possible sepulchre.

Catherine felt deeply the luke-warm attitude of official France to the dead philosopher. She ordered Grimm to buy his complete library, and ordered a hundred copies of the definitive edition of his works "so that I can distribute them everywhere. I want people to study them, to learn them by heart, to feed their souls on them: this will develop citizens, men of genius, heroes and authors; it will bring forth a hundred thousand talents which might otherwise be lost in the dark night of ignorance . . ."She asked Grimm to buy Voltaire's chateeau-hermitage at Ferney, so that she might rebuild it in the park at Tsarskoe Selo. While he was negotiating this and other Voltairean purchases, Grimm came into posession of her letters to the sage, and urged her to publish them as "the best monument one could raise to your Majesty's glory." She refused, and went on refusing despite ingenious attemps on his part to force her hand.

Grimm was kept busy by Catherine's appetite for objects of art and vertu, and from time to time acted as forwarding agent for even human cargoes. Catherine imported brains as assiduously as she did objects; and sice the fame of her appetites spread far and wide, from far and wide came careerists of every kind who hoped to become either lovers or pensioners. One such was Cagliostro: but Catherine's interest in the new and curious was not sufficiently childlike to expose her to such a charlatan.

July 9th, 1781: Catherine to Grimm:

As you speak to me of the charlatan Cagliostro, I must tell you about him also. He came here describing himself as a Colonel in the Spanish service, and of Spanish birth, letting it be understood that he was a magician, capable of making spirits visible and holding them at his disposition. When I heard that, I said: this man has made a great mistake to have come here—nowhere will he succeed less than in Russia. M. Cagliostro nevertheless came at a moment quite favourable for him; at a moment when several lodges of Freemasons, infatuated with the theories of Swedenborg, wished by whatever means they might to see spirits. He claimed to have extracted quicksilver from the foot of a gouty subject, and was caught in the act of dropping a spoonful of quicksilver in the water into which he had put this person. Then he produced dyes which would not dye, and chemical operations which did not operate. At last, crippled with debt, he took refuge in the cellar of M. Yelaguine (director of the court theatre), where he drank as much champagne and English beer as he could ... Such is the story of Cagliostro, in which there are elements of everything but the miraculous. I have never seen him near or far, nor have I been tempted to see him, for I do not like charlatans at all.

Grimm had ordered a stutue of Peter the First for Catherine, and was curious to know how it looked; suggesting that it should face the Black Sea cost, so as to give colour to the somewhat dim-sighted aspect of the face.

December 10th, 1782: Catherine to Grimm:

Peter the First, when he was first on view in the open air, appeared to have an expression as light-hearted as it was noble; one would have said he was content enough with his works. For a long time I was unable to gaze at all fixedly at him; I felt a thrill of tenderness, and when I looked around I saw that everyone had tears in their eyes. His head was turned away from the Black Sea, but its expression suggeseted that he was not dim-sighted in any direction. He was too far away to speak to me, but seemed to me to have an air of satisfaction which I shared, and which encoufaged me to try to do better in the future, if I can.

Grimm sent Catherine all kind of news and gifts trivial as well as valuable: gossip about fashion and the latest crazes as well as medals and cameos for her collections.

March 9th, 1782: Catherine to Grimm:

I thank you for the pots of rouge with which you hoped to enrich my face, but when I went to use it I found it so dark that it gave me the look of a Fury; so you must excuse me if, in spite of its great vogue where you are, I cannot imitate or adopt this beautiful fashion.

December 19th, 1783: Catherine to Crimm:

On the subject of discoveries, I compliment you on the aerial cars which fly around your heads. When they are perfected, it will be very agreeable to make the voyage from here to Paris in three days. Your aerostatic balloon has rendered a service to the state: it seems that it has made people forget the mistakes made in calculating the budget.

May 8th, 1784: Catherine to Grimm:

Did you ever think I would be foolish enough to forbid globes, balloons etc., from fear that one might increase the dangers of fire in a country where there are so many buildings and roofs in wood and straw?... Tell me the truth: in Paris you must have a new folly every month to take the place of the puppets, forbidden, so they tell me, under a law of Louis XV...

Houdon's bust of Voltaire arrived in the spring of this year, and was given a place of honour among Catherine's collection of statuary.

May 19th, 1784: Catherine to Grimm:

Listen, scape-goat, what I have to tell you. The statue of Voltaire made by Houdon was unpacked and placed in the Morning Room, where it is flanked by the Antinous, the Belvedere Apollo, and a number of other statues which

have come as moulds from Rome and which have been cast
here. When you enter the salon you literally catch your
breath; and—wonder of wonders—the statue of Voltaire
by Houdon is not at all disfigured by what surrounds it.
Voltaire is well placed there; he contemplates all that is
most beautiful in ancient and modern sculpture . . .

Towards the end of her correspondence with Baron
Grimm, Catherine becomes more serious in outlook.
Personal sorrows, and the events of the French revolution, weigh more heavily on her mind and she is given
more largely to reflective passages in which the con-
flict between the emotional woman and the pragmati-
cal pupil of Voltaire and other philosophers is clearly
visible. Faced with the death of a dear one, Lamskoy,
she begins to fear death herself.

Perhaps this sad event was a hint to Catherine that
even an Empress, with unlimited wealth and power at
her command, cannot influence the stars in her favour.
What she wanted, both for herself and for the world
in general, was a planned and genial existence; and
since her motives, both personal and political, were so
progressive and morally defensible, surely it was not
asking too much of events to fit in with the pattern
she had prescribed for them. But events, then as now,
had a habit of springing from causes. The changes in
French society, and the oppressions which led those
changes to explode in a greater and fundamental
change, were inevitable. Catherine may have believed
that her "Grand Instructions" would prevent revolution at home. She was powerless to prevent it abroad:
and instead of welcoming the upsurge of libertarian
ideas, she opposed and regretted it.

June 25, 1790: Catherine to Grimm:

Since in France you have agreed that further agreement is impossible, your country has lost its greatest attribute. What a fall is there! Brambles will grow on the highways again: Sully used to rejoice that his dear Henri IV had made them disappear. The next thing is for the National Assembly to order to be burned all the best French authors and everything that has spread your tongue abroad in Europe: for they all testify against the abominable squabbles they carry on. Until now one regarded as worthy of the gallows a man who put his mind to compassing the ruin of a country; and here is a whole nation, or rather 1,200 of its deputies, who are busying themselves with it. If you hanged one or two of them I think the rest would change their minds.

September 12, 1790: Catherine to Grimm:

Let us be frank; the prevailing tone of your country is the tone of the blackguard; it was not in such an atmosphere that France became illustrious, but certainly in that of the court of Louis XIV. What are the French going to do with their best authors? Even Voltaire—all of them are Royalists, they all preach order and tranquillity and everything that is opposed to the system of the 1,200-headed Hydra. Will they consign them to the flames?

April 30, 1791: Catherine to Grimm:

Do you know what will happen to France if you succeed in making it a republic? Everybody will want it to become a monarchy again. Believe me, nobody is happier at Court than the republican. From what I see and hear of France, she seems to me to be like a person sick in the soul; but her fickleness should make this malady pass more quickly with her than with any other nation seized with the same epidemic. It is an illness she catches every two hundred years. Look at her history.

December 6th, 1793: Catherine to Grimm:

I do not believe I have ever told you, though I have certainly felt it, that I am very sorry you should have been ruined by regicide rebels because they knew you were attached to me. But consider for a moment how they treat even those from whom they derive their very existence, those who have served them throughout all their excesses —this Bailly the astronomer, this Condorcet and a thousand others. They only know how to rob and kill; but they will kill so many that they will be exterminated themselves: true, this will mend nothing and will save nothing but the future ...

Catherine believed in the future, and believed that a monarch could contribute more to it than a people. Looking back on her "Grand Instructions", we see them as an attempt to achieve the impossible; an attempt based on the notion that the servants of absolutism could be as liberally minded as the arch-absolutist herself.

FROM THE MEMOIRS OF PRINCESS DASHKOV

The Palace Revolution

The removal of the court to Peterhof and Oranienbaum, which took place around the middle of summer, gave me as much leisure as I could have wished, and since this relieved me of the Emperor's evening parties I did not dislike remaining in town. At that time the guards, learning that they were to be instantly shipped to Denmark, displayed marked symptoms of discontent and unrest. Moreover, there were rumours that the Empress's life was in danger —rumours that were to serve in bringing nearer the time when the Guards's services would be required at home. I charged some officers who shared our secret to tell these soldiers—whom they observed closely and could hardly restrain—that I was in daily contact with the Empress and undertook to let them know when the suitable moment for action would have arrived.

In other respects an ominous calm prevailed until June 27, the day that will remain forever memorable in the annals of my country—a day when the hearts of all conspirators trembled with alternating fear and hope, anxiety and delight. When I remember the events of that memorable day, a glorious revolution accomplished without a plan and with means hardly adequate to the result achieved; carried out by individuals whose views and ideas were as varied and contradictory as their characters—some of them hardly knew one another and are not worthy of being compared since they shared nothing but their common desire for a successful outcome—when I think of all this it is impossible not to see the hand of Providence which guides to success plans that may be vague and lacking in purpose. If the leaders of conspiracies were candidly to admit how much they owe to chance and opportunity for the success of their enterprises, they must abandon many pretensions to merits of their own. As for myself I honestly admit that although I was the first to believe in the success of our plot, to dethrone a monarch incapable of ruling, I was enabled neither by what history I had read nor by the glowing imagination of a girl of eighteen, to visualise events such as reality was to produce a few hours later.

It was on the afternoon of June 27 that Gregory Orlov came to inform me of the arrest of Captain Passek. He and Bredichin had visited me the night before in order to warn me of the danger to which we were exposed through the impatience of the soldiers, particularly of the grenadiers who, giving credence to the rumours concerning the Empress's jeopardy, were speaking openly against Peter III and demanded loudly to be led against the Holstein troops at Oranienbaum. To relieve the apprehensions of these two gentlemen, and in order to show them that I was not afraid, I asked them to tell the soldiers on my behalf that I had daily news from the Empress, who was in complete safety and under no kind of restraint at Peterhof, and that it was absolutely necessary that they should keep calm and await orders, otherwise the favourable moment for action might never come. Passek and Bredichin lost no time in giving the soldiers this message, but the prevailing confusion and tumult brought our secret to the knowledge of Voyekov, a Major in the Preobrazhensky Guards, who immediately

placed Passek under close arrest, thus by a seemingly un-
lucky but in reality most fortunate action speeding up the
discovery and culmination of our conspiracy.

When Orlov arrived with news of this arrest whose
grounds and details he knew not, Panin happened to be
with me. Either because of his natural indolence and laxity
of character, or because he wished to conceal from me the
imminence of danger, he seemed to view the event in less
serious a light than I did, discussing it with great compo-
sure as though it were the result of some indiscipline. I, on
the contrary, regarded it as the signal for some decisive
step, and although I failed to convince him we asked Orlov
to go at once to the regimental barracks and to ascertain
the details of Passek's arrest, whether he was being treated
as a prisoner of state or merely as detained for some in-
fraction of discipline; if the former were the case we asked
him to return with all the details he could discover and to
send his brother with a similar report to Panin.

When Orlov had gone I asked my uncle Panin to leave me,
pretending to be in need of rest. As soon as he was gone,
however, I donned a large male greatcoat and thus disguised walked on foot to Raslovlev's house. I had not gone
far when I saw a horseman coming towards me at a gallop.
I do not know what gave me the idea that it must be one
of the Orlovs, of whom I knew only Gregory, but my conviction was so strong that I had the courage of halting his
rush by calling out his name. The horseman stopped, and
when he heard who had called to him, said: "I was on my
way to you, Princess, to tell you that Passek is a prisoner
of state, guarded by two sentries outside his door and two
at each window. My brother is on his way to Panin, and
I have just informed Raslovlev."—"And is he much fright-
ened by this news?"—"Somewhat", he said, "but why are
you in the street, Madame? Allow me to escort you home."

PRINCESS DASHKOV

—"We are less under observation here than we would be in my house, surrounded by servants. But at this time a few words are enough. Go, tell Raslovlev, Lassunsky, Tchertkov and Bredichin to hasten without delay to their regiment, the Ismailov Guards, and to remain at their posts to receive the Empress on the outskirts of the city. Then do you or one of your brothers fly like lightning to Peterhof and entreat the Empress from me to get immediately into a post carriage which she will find in readiness, and to drive to the quarters of the Ismailov Guards. They are waiting to proclaim her sovereign and to escort her into the capital. Tell her that this step is so important that I would not delay the message by the few moments I would lose by returning to my home and writing it down, but that I implored you in the street to tell her and hasten her arrival. I may come to meet her myself."

As regards the post carriage referred to: the night before, following the visit of Passek and Bredichin and their report on the soldiers' impatience, I had thought it possible that they might not wait for orders to act, and had therefore written to Madame Shkurin, the wife of the Empress's valet, asking her to send her carriage with four post horses to Peterhof; there, it was to be held in readiness for the Empress, if her presence in Petersburg should be required. I realised how difficult, nay impossible it would have been to get hold of a carriage without Ismailov, the imperial Majordomo, learning of it—the man least likely to further the Empress's escape. Panin, believing a revolution to be both remote and uncertain, laughed at this precaution; but as events turned out—who knows if without that carriage we should ever have attained our object.

After parting from Orlov I returned home, but in such excitement that I had little inclination for a patient wait. I had ordered a complete suit of male attire that was to have been ready that night, but the tailor had not sent it. This was a great disappointment, since feminine dress imposed restraint. In order to elude the suspicion or curiosity of my domestics I went to bed, but was aroused an hour later by a loud knocking on my front door. I jumped from my bed and rushed into the next room, giving orders to admit whoever might be calling. There entered a young man I did not know, who introduced himself as the youngest of the Orlov brothers. He had come, he told me, to ask me if it was not too soon to send for the Empress who might be unnecessarily alarmed by a premature call to Petersburg. I would hear no more: my annoyance was at its peak, and I did not attempt to restrain my fury against his brothers for hesitating to carry out the orders (as I most ungracefully put it) I had given to Alexis Orlov. "You have wasted precious time", I said, "and as to your fears of alarming the Empress, let her be brought here in a faint rather than expose her to the danger of spending her life in prison or ending it on the scaffold with us. Tell your brother therefore to ride at the utmost speed to Peterhof and to bring the Empress to Petersburg without losing a moment, before Peter III receives intelligence, arrives here before her and frustrates a plan held out by Providence to save our country and the Empress."

He seemed impressed by my seriousness and left me with the assurance that his brother was going to comply with my instructions.

When he had left I became a prey to sombre reflections. Once immersed in such sad thoughts, none but horrid pictures formed in my mind. I longed to meet the Empress, but the aforementioned disappointment over my masculine clothes was an evil spell, confining me to the solitude and inactivity of my room. My ever active imagination would for some instants picture the Empress's triumph and the resultant happiness of my country; but these pleasant images were quickly dispelled by others that made me shudder with horror. The least noise terrified me: I pictured Catherine, the idol of my soul, pale, disfigured, dying, the victim of our rashness. At last this horrible night, which seemed like a lifetime of suffering, was over. But how am I to describe the delight with which I greeted that eventful morning when news reached me that the Empress had entered the capital and had been proclaimed sovereign by the Ismaïlov Guards whom she was even now leading to the Kazan Cathedral together with the military and citizenry of the town, all eager to swear the oath of allegiance.

It was six o'clock in the morning. I told my maid to bring me a gala dress and drove to the Winter Palace where I had correctly assumed Her Majesty would take up residence. It is difficult to describe how I got there. The Palace was surrounded and every entrance so blocked by soldiers who had rushed there from all parts of the town to cast in their lot with the Guards, that I had to step from my carriage and make my way on foot through the crowd. Hardly had some officers and men of the Guards recognized me when I felt borne up from the ground and quickly passed over the heads of the crowd who loudly cheered me as their friend and heaped a thousand blessings on me. When I was finally set down in some anteroom, my head giddy, my hair dishevelled, my dress torn and my whole attire disarranged, a token of my triumphant entry into the palace, I rushed to the Empress. In a moment we were in each other's arms. "Heaven be praised", was all we could utter in those first moments.

She then described to me her flight from Peterhof and her fears and hopes during the crisis. I listened, my heart racing, and in my turn told her of the anxious hours I had lived through, made more anxious by my inability to meet her (the reasons for which I explained) and to share with her those hours when her fate and the destiny of the country for good or evil were in the balance. Once again we embraced, and never was mortal more completely happy than I was then. Soon afterwards, seeing that Her Majesty was wearing the ribbon of the Order of St. Catherine but not yet that of St. Andrew, the highest order in the state which no woman could receive but of which, as sovereign, she was now Grand Master, I ran to Panin and fetched his blue ribbon, which I threw over her shoulder. When Her Majesty took off the Order of St. Catherine and gave it to me I put it in my pocket.

After a light repast Catherine proposed to move to Peterhof at the head of the troops. She wished me to accompany her. As she preferred to appear in Guards uniform she borrowed a uniform from Captain Talitzin whilst I, following her example, obtained one from Lieutenant Pushkin, two officers of about our size. These uniforms, by the way, were the old national uniform of the Preobrazhensky Guards as worn ever since the days of Peter I until it was ousted by the Prussian-style uniform introduced by Peter III. It is noteworthy that immediately after the Empress's entry in the city the Guards, as at one command, threw away their foreign costume and to the last man appeared in the old uniform of their country.

While the Empress retired in order to prepare for the expedition I hastened home to make the requisite alterations in my attire. When I returned to the Palace I found Her Majesty considering the manifestoes to be issued. She was surrounded by all the Senators who happened to be in the city, and in addition there was Teplov who had been asked to act as Secretary.

As by this time the news of the Empress's flight from Peterhof and of subsequent happenings in town must have reached Oranienbaum, I was struck by the thought that Peter III, acting on bold and quick advice, might make a rapid move and appear before Petersburg to quell the rising of the troops. Giving in to an impulse I decided to tell the Empress. The two officers guarding the door of the Council Chamber who had instructions to admit no one opened the door and let me in, probably thinking I had a special permit. I hastened to Her Majesty and in a whisper told her of the thought that had caused my intrusion; I begged her to use all means to prevent Peter's arrival. Teplov was immediately ordered to draw up a ukase and send copies, together with further orders, to two bodies of troops who were to occupy the still unguarded approaches to the town from the sea. The Empress, noticing the astonishment of the venerable senators at my appearance—for none of them recognised me in my disguise—told them who I was, and that it was to my ever faithful friendship that she owed an essential precaution she had overlooked. The Senators rose to a man from their seats to salute me, a sign of respect that made me blush and abashed, for it little became me to have intruded in this guise, as a boy in military uniform, and to have whispered into the Empress's ear with such lack of respect.

Soon afterwards, the meeting being over and the orders necessary for the safety of the capital having been given, we mounted our horses and on our way to Peterhof passed in review twelve thousand troops, not counting volunteers whose numbers increased every minute.

At Krasnoy Kabak, ten versts from Petersburg, we halted for some hours so as to provide some rest for the troops who had been on their feet for twelve hours. We needed rest ourselves: for the past two weeks I had hardly ever closed my eyes. When we entered our miserable little hovel Her Majesty proposed that we should lie down in our clothes on the one small bed that was in the room and which, dirty as everything was, seemed too alluring to be rejected by our tired limbs. We had hardly lain down on the bed—which I took care first to cover with a cloak borrowed from Colonel Karr—when I noticed a small door in the wall behind the Empress's bolster. As I did not know whither it led I asked for permission to go outside and inspect everything for security. When I found that this door gave on a dark, narrow passage leading to the outer courtyard, I posted two sentries there with orders not to move from the spot without my instructions. When this was done I went back to the Empress. I found her busy reading papers, and as we were unable to sleep she read to me the manifestoes she was going to publish. We had leisure to consider what remained to be done, and were now full of good cheer which had taken the place of our former apprehensions.

Abdication and death of Peter III

During all this time Peter III, refusing to follow General Münnich's advice, was unable to make up his mind. He travelled to and fro between Peterhof and Oranienbaum until he saw that this would not profit him, whereupon he followed his friends' advice and set out for Kronstadt to make sure of the navy. The Empress, however, had also not overlooked the importance of the navy. She had sent Admiral Talitzin to command it in her name. When he, having occupied Kronstadt, saw the Czar approaching the shore he would not let him land. Hapless Peter was compelled to return to Oranienbaum. He sent General Ismaïlov to the Empress with the humblest declarations and an offer of abdication.

The bearer of these proposals found us on our way to Peterhof; how different were his language and behaviour from those of my uncle, the Chancellor, who had just presented himself before the Empress prior to our leaving town. He had come to reason with the Empress. When he saw that his objections remained ineffective he withdrew them but refused to make oath of allegiance. "Rest assured, Madame", he said with the calm dignity of a great soul, "that I shall never try to harm your government by word or deed; and in order to prove my sincerity I suggest that some of your loyal officers guard my house. But I will never break the oath I have sworn to the Czar as long as he lives."

Her Majesty sent General Ismaïlov back to Peter III, having implored him to induce the Emperor to place himself in her hands in order to prevent the incalculable ills that might result from any other line of conduct; she added her solemn promise that she was going to do everything to render his life as pleasant as possible at some residence a certain distance from Petersburg, which he might choose himself.

As we were approaching the Monastery of the Holy Trinity, Vice-Chancellor Prince Galitzin came with a letter from the Czar, whilst the crowd around us grew every moment with fresh numbers of opponents of the Czar.

Soon after our arrival at Peterhof it was reported that Peter III, accompanied by Generals Ismaïlov and Gudovitch, had arrived at the palace and surrendered. Hardly noticed by anyone, he was taken to a remote room where a meal stood ready; and as he had chosen for his residence the castle of Ropcha where he had been living when Grand Duke, he was immediately taken thither. With him went Alexis Orlov, Captain Passek, Prince Fedor Bariatinsky, and Lieutenant Baskakov, of the Preobrazhensky Regiment, all of whom the Empress had entrusted with the care of Peter's person.

I did not see him in this catastrophe, though I could have

done so; but those who saw him assured me that he seemed hardly affected by this change in his fortunes. Before leaving Peterhof he sent two or three little notes to the Empress. In one of them, which I chanced to see, he declared his abdication in plain terms, and after having named several persons whose company he desired he spoke of the manner in which provision was to be made for his table, not forgetting to ask for large supplies of Burgundy, pipes and tobacco.

But enough of this unfortunate prince whom nature had formed for the lowest station in life while Fate unluckily raised him to a throne. Though he could not be described as vicious, his failings, his lack of education and his natural propensity for everything vile and common would have been no less pernicious to his people than downright vice, had he continued to rule.

Throughout that day I did not find a moment's rest, but my mind and inclination were so much concerned with the happenings of the moment that I did not feel the slightest fatigue until I ceased to be active.

That evening I was busied with various things, now at this end of the palace, now at the other, now with the sentries guarding the various entrances. When I brought a request from the Princess of Holstein, a relative of the Empress's, to be admitted by her—what was my astonishment at beholding Gregory Orlov stretched at full length on a sofa in one of the rooms (having hurt his leg, it appeared) with a large packet of papers before him which he was in the act of opening and which I recognised as state papers, messages from the Senate such as I had seen at my uncle's during Elizabeth's reign. I asked him in amazement what he was doing. "The Empress has ordered that I should open them", he answered. "That is impossible", I said, "she could not want them to be opened before officially appointing the persons who are to deal with their contents, and for this task you can consider yourself no more adequate than I could myself."

At this point we were interrupted by a report that the soldiers encamped about the palace, plagued by great thirst after the day's exertions, had broken into the cellars and were draining the casks of Hungarian wine in the belief that it was a kind of hydromel, the common drink of the country. I immediately went out to remonstrate with them at this violation of discipline, and to my great saticfaction and surprise—for officers' orders were being disregarded in the general confusion—my address was so successful that they threw away all the wine which they still had in their helmets, rolled the casks back into their places, and were content to slake their thirst at the nearest well. I gave them all the money I had with me and then turned my pockets inside out to show them that I had done everything in my capacity to gratify them. I promised them that when we returned to town the inns would be thrown open, and they could drink their fill at the expense of the crown. This kind of rhetoric was entirely to their taste, and they dispersed in the utmost good humour.

In mentioning this incident I am reminded of having read in certain books that I was supposed to have received money from the Empress and from foreign courts in support of our revolutionary activities, an assertion which I wish to refute at this juncture. I have never demanded or received a single rouble from Her Majesty; and while the French Ambassador offered me unlimited credits my reply had always been that no foreign monies were going to be used with my approval to further our revolution.

When on my way back to the Empress I passed through the same room where I had seen Gregory Orlov stretched out on the sofa, I noticed that a table with three covers had been laid. Dinner was announced, and the Empress invited me to share her repast. When we entered the room I noticed with extreme disapprobation that the table had been moved in front of the couch on which Orlov was lying. This disapprobation must have become manifest in my face, for Her Majesty asked me if anything was the matter. "Nothing", I replied, "besides loss of sleep and extreme exhaustion for fourteen nights."

She then tried to get me on her side in an argument with Orlov who wanted to resign from the service. "Consider", she said, "how ungrateful I should look if I allowed him to retire now." My answer did not, I think, come up to her expectations, for I said that as his sovereign she had so many means of rewarding him that there was no need to do violence to his wishes.

A conviction now for the first time forced itself upon my mind that was extremely painful and humiliating. It was evident that there was a liaison between them. After the meal and Peter's departure we set out for Petersburg, resting on the way for two hours in a country house belonging to Prince Kurakin, where the Empress and I again used the only available bed. Thence we repaired to Katharinenhof, where our appearance was acclaimed by an incredible throng of people.

To describe the scene that now ensued is beyond my powers. As we entered the capital and progressed in triumph, all streets, all windows were crowded with people whose cheers for the Empress filled the air, whilst the bands of all regiments were playing and the peals of church bells added to the joyous clamour that surrounded our cavalcade. The gates of the churches stood open, and at their candle-decked altars priests could be seen blessing with the ceremonies of religion the joy of the people.

When we reached the gates of the Summer Palace I felt

completely exhausted by the rapid sequence of events; and as I was eager to learn of their effect on my father and my uncle and wished to see my child, I asked for Her Majesty's permission to use her coach for this purpose. Having left her with the promise of an early return, I first drove to the house of my uncle, which was nearest. I found this truly venerable man his usual self, quiet and dignified as ever. He spoke of Peter's dethronement as an event he had been expecting; but the chief topic of his conversation was the danger of putting too much trust in the friendship of princes which, as he had seen on many occasions, was neither lasting nor sincere. He assured me that he had learned from experience how the purest of motives and the most honourable conduct were no protection against the effects of jealousy and intrigue, even in the proximity of a queen who was grateful for services rendered, and to whom he had been devoted from early youth ...

As I returned to the palace and was entering the anteroom leading to Her Majesty's apartments, I saw Gregory Orlov and Kakavinsky coming out. As soon as I saw the Empress it was evident that Orlov was my enemy, for none but he could have introduced Kakavinsky to the Empress. She reprimanded me for having tried to remove the soldiers from their post [her father's house which Kakavinsky had occupied with a squad of soldiers] and of having spoken in French to this officer in their presence. My answer was brief and accompanied by an expression which was bound to show her how this kind of reception affected me. I said: "Many hours have not elapsed since Your Majesty has ascended the throne, and in this short period I have received such proofs of the soldiers' confidence that what I say will not offend them, whatever language may be spoken." And in order to end the conversation I handed her the red ribbon of the order. "Softly, softly", she replied, "surely you must admit that you ought-not to have dismissed the soldiers from their post."—"Indeed", I said, "instead of complying with Vadkovsky's orders [for reinforcements] I suppose I should have allowed that fool Kakavinsky to do what he pleased and leave Your Majesty without a relief of guards for the protection of the palace."—"There, there," said she, "what I said was for your rashness: this is for your services", and she threw the ribbon of the Order of St. Catherine over my shoulder. Instead of receiving it on my knees, I retorted: "Your Majesty will pardon me for saying that the time seems already to have come when truth must be banished from your presence. May I beg you not to give me this decoration which as an ornament I do not esteem and which as a reward is of no value to one whose services, however highly they may be valued by some people, never have been nor shall be bought." She embraced me affectionately and said: "Friendship, at least, has some rights, and will you not allow me to enjoy its pleasure at this moment?" Instead of a reply I kissed her hand.

There I stood, in military uniform, the red ribbon without the star over my shoulder, booted and spurred and looking like a lad of fifteen.

Her Majesty then told me that she had ordered a Guards lieutenant to be despatched to Prince Dashkov in order to recall him to Petersburg as soon as possible. This proof of affection, and at such a moment, delighted me so much that my annoyance was quickly forgotten. She also told me that instructions had been given for rooms to be held in readiness for us at the palace, which would be ready for me on the morrow; but I begged permission to decline this, so that on my husband's return we could occupy them together.

About an hour later, when everybody retired, I hurried

home and after sharing supper with my little Natasha I went to bed. Yet the excitement of my mind, combined with the exhaustion of my soul and body, made me incapable of sound sleep. I passed the night in a feverish doze, interrupted by wild imaginings and nervous starts.

On the following day Panin received the title of Count with a pension of 5,000 roubles; Prince Volkonsky and Count Razumovsky received the same pension; the other leading conspirators each 600 peasants and 2,000 roubles pension, or 24,000 roubles in lieu of serfs. To my greatest astonishment I found my name in this list, but I was resolved to make no use of the gift. For this disinterestedness I received the reproaches of all who had taken part in the revolution. My friends soon changed their tune, however, and in the end, in order to put an end to the argument and not to offend the Empress, I consented to a compromise. I had a list of my husband's debts, totalling almost 24,000 roubles: I made over to his creditors the draft on the Privy Purse I had been given.

On the fourth day after the revolution Monsieur Betskoy demanded an audience and was admitted. I happened to be alone with the Empress when he entered and to our great surprise fell on his knees while adjuring the Empress to confess to whose influence she owed her accession to the throne. "To Almighty God," she said, "and to the choice of my subjects."—"Then", he said in despair, "I must no longer wear this ribbon", and made to tear off his ribbon of the Order of St. Alexander when the Empress stopped him and asked him what on earth he was referring to.

"I am the unhappiest of men", he said, "if Your Majesty fails to recognize in me the only person to whom you owe your crown. Have I not been inciting the Guards? Have I not been distributing money among the people?"

We both thought he had gone mad and began to feel somewhat apprehensive when the Empress with her habitual adroitness found a witty expedient to rid us of this extraordinary persecution and at the same time give full satisfaction to his vanity. With the greatest seriousness she said: "I admit the full extent of my obligation, and as it is to your efforts that I owe the crown, who could be better suited to make the one I am going to wear at my coronation? To you therefore I entrust this matter and am placing you in charge of all jewellers in my realm."

Betskoy rose with the greatest delight and after thanking her a thousand times rushed out of the chamber, presumably in order to spread the news of the reward he had received for his services. Needless to say, we heartily laughed over this incident which was as characteristic of the Empress's quickness of mind as it was of Betskoy's folly.

At that juncture the court of Petersburg furnished particular interest: the revolution had caused new faces to emerge while numerous people of note who had been banished during the period of Empress Anna, Biron's regency and the reign of Elizabeth were returning daily. Many of them had held high office and knew the secrets of earlier governments; their misfortunes had been part of ancient days and served as objects of curiosity or to point a moral —and all these people were suddenly, after years of obscurity and political death, re-emerging into the sunshine of political importance.

At last the former Chancellor, Bestushev, also made his appearance. The Empress presented me to him in a special manner, using such terms as to torment the Orlovs. "This is young Princess Dashkov", she said, "would you credit that it is the daughter of Count Roman Voronzov to whom I owe the throne?"

I had seen Bestushev only once, four years earlier and at a distance. At that time I was struck by the intelligence of his face and on enquiring was for the first time told that famous man's name. I am mentioning this because in some accounts of the revolution I am accused of having conspired against Peter III with him, although I was not yet fourteen at the time of his banishment. So great is the disregard for truth and the ignorance of facts displayed in the works of some French writers that one might believe them in a conspiracy to deprive history of all value and instruction by filling their pages with senseless calumnies and silly lies.

In this universal resurrection two other famous men took part, Field-Marshal Münnich and Lestocq. I remember having seen them at my uncle's when I was a child: he loved both of them. Marshal Münnich, now aged eighty-four, was distinguished by great courtesy which contrasted not a little with the uncouth manners of some of our conspirators. He had lost none of his remarkable firmness of character and was still in full possession of his faculties. His conversation was extremely interesting to me, and I still feel proud that in his kindness he gave me frequent occasion to enjoy it. I regarded these two men as the living chronicles of past days, and as I reflected on this twofold world of the past and the present I began to understand things better, though my inexperience still deceived me with youthful hopes of building a temple of all the virtues in the human heart.

But in the midst of the reflections induced by all these interesting events my thoughts were suddenly taken up by a dreadful reality that filled me with consternation and terror—the tragic end of Peter III. I was so indignant at this news, so furious at this outcome of our glorious revolution that, whilst rejecting the idea of the Empress's complicity in the crime committed by Alexei Orlov, I could not bring myself to set foot in the palace before the following day. I found the Empress looking greatly disturbed and obviously deeply moved. She addressed these words to me: "My horror at this death is unutterable, it is a blow that fells me to the ground."—I replied: "It is too quick a death for your glory and for mine, Madame."

No other thought entered my mind. In the course of the evening I was rash enough to say in the presence of many people that I hoped Alexis Orlov would now realise more than ever that we were not made to breathe the same air. I was proud enough to believe that he was in future not going to greet me even as an acquaintance. From this day the Orlovs became my sworn enemies and in justice to Alexei I must admit that in spite of his innate impudence he never, during the following twenty years, dared address a word to me.

Anyone malignant enought to accuse the Empress of participation in, or even foreknowledge of, her husband's assassination, will find absolute proof of the unfairness of such suspicion in a letter that is still extant and which was written in Alexis Orlov's own hand a few moments after the horrible deed had been done. Its style and incoherence show clearly, despite his drunkenness, the terror and wildness of his fears while he solicits pardon for his act in the most supplicatory terms.

Catherine preserved this important letter with great care in a casket containing other important papers. After her death Prince Bezhborodko was ordered by Paul to examine the contents of the casket and read them out in his presence. When he had finished reading the letter of Alexis Orlov Paul made the sign of the cross and exclaimed: "God be praised! The few doubts of my mother that I still entertained in this respect are now dissolved."—The Czarina and Demoiselle Nelidov were present, and the Czar ordered the letter to be read out to the Grand Duke and Count Rostopchin as well.